# ENDORSEMENTS FOR
# *OUT INTO THE DESERT*

"This book reminded me of all the joys and sorrows, the pains and pleasures, the ups and downs, the ins and outs, and the beauties and complexities of ministry together. It reminded me of how two quite different people can lovingly work together on the same team. And it also reminded me of why we left the ministry together and wandered into our own desert that's now become an oasis."

DAVID HAYWARD, AKA NAKEDPASTOR

"Whether we are drawn into the desert by love, or pushed there by difficulties, the desert proves to be a more refreshing place than we ever imagined. Karl and Laura Forehand offer a glimpse of this reality in their lives. May it empower you to take the next step toward authenticity in your own journey."

BEN DELONG, AUTHOR OF *BECOMING HOME*

"In this book, Karl and Laura begin with their Christian roots, break up the soil of organized religion, and sprout fruiting flowers that give spiritually nourishing food to the readers. Nothing is off limits in this book."

DERRICK DAY, CO-HOST OF FREEOLOGYFRIDAY

"Laura and Karl recount their experiences with the institutional church to capture what so many people experience: *disillusionment, pain, and frustration*. Their testimonies are not only moving, but also instructive."

THOMAS JAY OORD, AUTHOR OF *OPEN AND RELATIONAL THEOLOGY* AND OTHER BOOKS

"Many of us are on a spiritual journey with no known destination. Karl and Laura Forehand have been there and share their transparency and wisdom with us in the pages of *Out Into the Desert*. Their only agenda is to help us know that we're not alone and that this desert isn't as barren as it initially appears."

JASON ELAM, CO-HOST OF MESSY SPIRITUALITY

"Karl and Laura Forehand's *Out Into the Desert* is a wonderful choreography that displays a beautiful and courageous dance between their vulnerable inner lives and their outer experiences with toxic theology and the failings of the church. They also offer liberative pathways and principles that will guide readers toward a more honest spirituality leading to healthier and life-giving connections."

MARK KARRIS, AUTHOR OF *RELIGIOUS REFUGEES: (DE) CONSTRUCTING TOWARD SPIRITUAL AND EMOTIONAL HEALING*

"Certainty, not doubt, is the opposite of faith and life abundant awaits after leaving certainty behind. Karl and Laura speak from their pain, their fear of stepping away from all they held to be certain, and the hope they have found in the desert. This is a story that invites each of us to step into the desert for the freedom and peace that awaits in authentic community."

GREG WEATHERD, A FELLOW DESERT NOMAD

"A must-read book that examines the journey from leadership in evangelical Christianity to leaving the organized institutional church. Their journey into the desert took them from shallow, pat answers, to asking profound questions. They find the desert encouraging and well worth the time it takes to take this journey."

JOE MACHUTA, ARTIST AND BLOGGER

"Karl and Laura Forehand explore and normalize the exit journey familiar to those of us who have left the building for something seemingly unstructured and wilderness-like. They examine ways of thinking about organized religion, and ask honest, pragmatic questions about 'church modus operandi.' Karl and Laura's book is a companion guide on this journey that provides insight and support. The Forehand's shared dialogue reminds us that we are not alone, and the desert is a beautiful place; habitable and very much alive."

ELLEN COMPTON, AUTHOR OF *GOOD THINGS HAPPEN IN THE DARK: A CANDID MANIFESTO FOR COURAGEOUS AUTHENTICITY*

"Karl has long had a penchant for bringing light to the forgotten postures of faith. This time, he's joined by his wife Laura, and their voices together speak truth to different sides of the same coin, from surviving church ministry to wandering and embracing the vulnerable ways of Christ. This book spoke deeply to my soul, as it will yours."

STUART DELONEY, HOST OF SNARKY FAITH RADIO

"Brave authentic questioning with humility and sensitivity, give place to God purifying everything that matters. In *Out Into the Desert*, Karl and Laura conduct a masterful and sensitive exploration into where, how, and if the church organizational structure, as we have known it, fits into the lives of believers, who are hungering to grow in life, love, character, community, service, and calling. They do this with an authenticity that gives permission to question, grapple, and heal from structures that have all too often proved oppressive or downright toxic. Their work is brave, refreshing, and humble, even as it asks tough questions. Their experience in a 20-year pastoral/pastoral spouse calling gives their perspectives unique validity and insight. I can heartily recommend *Out Into the Desert* to anyone reevaluating the place that church as usual holds!"

CATHERINE TOON, MD, AUTHOR, SPEAKER, AND COACH

"For those deconstructing (evolving), it is the logical structure built around our embodied spiritual awareness that falls away. The 3rd century Desert Fathers and Mothers left the corrupting power structures of the institutional church to keep alive a deeply embodied spirituality. The desert is not a bad place, and you are not alone. Karl and Laura's very honest book describes much of my wounding experience as pastor in several churches. They describe it well."

DR. PAUL D. FITZGERALD, CO-FOUNDER
OF HEARTCONNEXION SEMINARS

"*Out Into the Desert* asks all the questions many, if not most of us, have asked during our faith journey. We are given permission to explore the fallibility of the church, to exhume the skeleton of the Gospel, to call forth the winds of truth and the Father's true intent for the Body. It is the innocence of honesty that sets this book apart. It is the clarity of soul expressed by Karl and Laura that serve to break the addiction to church and develop something deeper. *Out Into the Desert* is so much more than a book worth reading, it is a journey worth taking!"

DESIMBER ROSE WATTLETON, AUTHOR OF
*THE CHURCH CAN GO TO HELL*

# OUT INTO THE DESERT

*Thriving Outside Organized Religion*

Heidi
Be where you are
Be who you are
Be at peace!

KARL *and* LAURA FOREHAND

First Edition

Cover design and layout by Rafael Polendo (polendo.net)
Cover image by Yothakan Thuphom (shutterstock.com)



ISBN 978-1-957007-23-6

This volume is printed on acid free paper and meets ANSI Z39.48 standards.

Printed in the United States of America

Published by Quoir
Oak Glen, California

www.quoir.com

DEDICATED TO

Every person who,
like the prophets and mystics before them,
found courage and followed their inner voice
toward what was calling them,
even when it cost them greatly.

# TABLE OF CONTENTS

# FOREWORD

There's nothing in this book you don't already know in your bones.

That's not to say you won't learn anything new by reading it, or that what Karl and Laura have written here isn't worth your time or attention.

On the contrary, it's precisely because you already know the same pain, struggle, doubt, anxiety, fear, and loneliness they speak of in these pages that this book will become more precious, necessary, and healing for you.

Because you know this desert well, you've become accustomed to wandering alone where there is no path, no marker, no landmark, and no guidepost to point the way. You're familiar with the feelings of isolation as those who once called you "brother" or "sister," suddenly pretend not to recognize you at the grocery store. You've known the anguish of doubt, as the faith that once comforted you, suddenly evaporates in the heat of unanswered questions.

None of us finds ourselves in this desert because we wanted to be here. No, we never set out to make our home in this wasteland. We merely asked a question, which turned into another question, and before we knew it, we were told to keep quiet, to stop rocking the boat, and then, eventually, to leave—either because they couldn't tolerate our doubt, or because we couldn't bear to listen to their toxic theology for one more minute.

Either way, we found ourselves spiritually homeless, wandering like nomads in a desert of uncertainty, searching for an oasis of truth and, who knows, maybe even a tribe that welcomes our questions and embraces our uncertainty.

If any of this resonates with you, let me be the first to inform you: *you are not alone*. There are hundreds of thousands—perhaps millions—of people just like you all around the globe who have pulled those same threads, asked the same questions, removed the same Jenga pieces, and watched their entire spiritual identity unravel, collapse, and vanish like a mist.

Still, the fact that, statistically, there are innumerable nomads wandering this desert somewhere out there does nothing to comfort you here and now. You're still the only person you know in your zip code who knows what it's like to be who you are now, and to be where you are at this moment.

That's why this book, and others like it, are so important. Because they serve as necessary reminders that, while we feel so alone, we are actually surrounded by a great cloud of witnesses who understand our pain and have walked this path before us.

Karl and Laura are both wise, experienced guides for the journey you find yourself on at this moment. They have walked this path and found hope when it wasn't easy to find. They've struggled, suffered, wept, given up, walked away, fallen down, and then, when anyone else would have given up in despair, they found the inner resolve to keep going, and keep searching for hope when there was simply no good reason to do so.

I'll bet you know what that's like. I'm sure you know how it feels. I know I do. My wife, Wendy, and I have felt called to follow the Spirit out into the desert—into the great unknown—and we've wandered out into the darkness, not sure of where we were going, but certain that where we were wasn't home, and where we'd been wasn't right for us. That holy discontent drove us out of our comfort zones, away from our paid church staff positions, and out where all we had were questions and not as many answers.

The good news is, we found our way. Karl and Laura did, too. You'll make it, just as we did, by learning to listen to the voice of the Spirit, ignoring the naysayers and the cynics who try to discourage you, and setting your face towards the polar north star that pulls on that invisible compass needle somewhere deep in your chest.

You know the one. That irresistible yearning for truth that you cannot let go of, and that will not—ever—let you go; it calls to you, it knows your name, it seeks you, it draws you, inevitably, out into the desert, out where every mystic, and prophet, and messiah has always felt drawn.

In these pages you will hear echoes of truth that vibrate with the frequency of your inner tuning fork. You will find yourself nodding along with the words you read. You will hear your own inner voice ringing in unison with theirs in these pages.

Best of all, you'll realize that it's possible to not only survive this journey, but to actually thrive.

Welcome to the desert, my friends. We're glad you're here.

**—Keith Giles**
Bestselling author of the 7-part *Jesus Un* series
El Paso, TX

# INTRODUCTION

Several years ago, I went through what most people call a deconstruction of some of my religious beliefs. It started as moving from a fundamentalist, evangelical system to a more Christ-like, less retributive view of God. I first compared my beliefs about God to my experience as a parent. I wrote a book called *Apparent Faith: What Fatherhood Taught Me About the Father's Heart*. It became a journal of my journey through deconstruction, and I was pleased to share that part of my heart with the world.

I discovered that when I changed my beliefs it made some people uncomfortable, and it felt like I was wandering out into the desert. I didn't want that to happen. I didn't want to lose a bunch of friends but separating from systems and people made it feel like I was leaving everything behind. I couldn't really be a preacher or traditional pastor anymore, but I was determined to find some community out here in the wilderness. To my surprise, there were more people than I would have imagined, and through our website and Facebook communities, we were able to connect with others and walk together through this time.

So, why would I write this book? As I began to examine my beliefs, Laura and I continued to go to church. Little by little, even in a couple of good churches, we began to feel increasingly out of place. Eventually, we stopped going to church and began to think through why we no longer wanted to go.

I want to examine two things in this book. First, I want to see if it is possible to survive, or even thrive, outside of organizational religion. People have told me that it is, but I want to know for myself. We experienced a fair amount of pain in church, and we aren't anxious to go back, even though people have encouraged us to return. People have also welcomed us out into the desert. I was warned that I would lose my faith, but I felt like I was drowning anyway, so I wanted to find out if it's possible to thrive here.

The second thing I want to examine is what needs to change about the church. Most of the issues I found on the outside looking in were obscured when I was inside the church. It makes sense now, but I couldn't see it on the inside, especially when I was employed by a church. I have chosen to interweave these two things, and just imagine and examine them as they come to me. That means that there may be some overlap and I may even change my mind later in this manuscript.

I invite you to come along on this journey with me. Like many of my most respected friends, I am thankful for some of the things the church as an organization has given me, but it needs to be reimagined as we move swiftly into the future. It doesn't need to be like it was and it doesn't have to stay like it is. Change is hard, but change is often necessary. Let us examine it together!

Laura has agreed to help me in this process. She is a good writer, but she only writes when she feels inspired. Her input is vital to this journey because her voice was held in check by the systems that we were in. Her voice is particularly important as we journey forward. Come along with us—we look forward to hearing your voice one day.

**—Karl Forehand**

2020

PART 1

# *Some Observations About Church*

# 1

# THE MAIN THING

## *Karl*

I am fairly sure I heard the phrase first from one of my mentors, although I very well could have heard it in a secular boardroom. It goes something like this:

*"We have to keep the main thing the main thing."*

This statement is a little more than establishing goals, or even priorities. The phrase is used to declare what is most important in an organization. In churches, the phrase is used to motivate people to action and keep them focused on value-added activities. What is the thing we should think about the most, so that we do what is most important, instead of what feels natural for us to do (what feels good)? What would bring the most return for our efforts and/or be the most Scriptural or most Christlike? In my opinion, the struggle with this idea is not necessarily the initial answer to the question. The problem is what eventually becomes the main thing in most American churches.

For most evangelical churches, the obvious "main thing" would be *evangelism.* I even used to say, "unless our church is evangelistic, then we are not a church." This focus is an attempt to respond to Jesus' injunction to fulfill the Great Commission to "go and make disciples."[1] We have differing ideas about what this actually means, but most churches would probably agree that this is the main thing! Again, the problem is not the initial intent—the issue is what the intent becomes.

When an organization decides to grow, it is about inevitable that the main thing becomes attracting new membership and retaining those that are already on board. Once the group has any kind of volume, it is very natural to focus on membership growth, budgets to maintain the organization, and strategies to make the membership productive and happy. There are always champions of noble causes, but the business of running a church demands that there always be new, potential members coming in the front door. It's very much like running any other business. We even call them prospects when we talk about them in strategy meetings. Potential members need a place to park, adequate restrooms, and a place to drop off their toddler (we call it *parking, preschool and potties*—the holy trinity of church growth)!

Most of the staff in a typical church is postured toward the potential church members. Generally, there are specific people to greet new members. Many churches have follow-up plans to reach out to those that filled out a visitor card. Let me be clear, I don't think there is anything wrong with being hospitable and making people feel welcome. But, in our attempts to grow the organization, has the *main thing* really gotten lost in the shuffle?

---

**1** Matthew 28:19–20

The church is described as a family, but what if we are neglecting the current family because we're always searching for the next addition to our clan? What if the lost sheep is really within the people that already attend? What if the most recent drop in membership is due to a valid problem in the organization that we don't have time to address? What if the wounded are hobbling out one door as we greet new members coming in the other?

It is probably safe to say that a certain number of people will leave the organized church on a regular basis, and some will never return.[2] Especially when churches are seeker-sensitive and longing to attract new members, people will always act like consumers and "shop around" for what suits them best. I certainly had my share of disappointment toward people that left the church without explanation. But is the answer to this modern dilemma to just keep feeding people into the machine? Should we neglect current members and write off the ones that are leaving since it's "inevitable" anyway? Or should we take a long hard look at what business as usual looks like in the 21$^{st}$ century church?

I don't do very well at malls. There is a flurry of activity and too many distractions that keep me from my objective of getting what I came for in the first place. I like specialized stores and places where I can get what I already researched. When we go grocery shopping, we like to have a list, otherwise we leave the store spending way too much money and, often, not getting what we really needed. Most churches are trying to find the moving target of what people want. They spend lots of money, read lots of books, and gather at conferences to hear the latest strategies. My previous denomination was obsessively focused

---

2 https://www.pewforum.org/2012/10/09/nones-on-the-rise/

on what would appeal to the current church prospects, but ultimately, spent very little time respectively on member care.

You see, the other thing Jesus said very strongly often gets lost in the shuffle. It is called "The Great Commandment." He said it is the embodiment of all the law and the prophets. It is the most important thing we can do. By doing it, we will fulfill our purpose—it is indeed "The main thing." When the Pharisees asked Jesus what the main thing was, he replied,

> "YOU SHALL LOVE THE LORD YOUR GOD WITH ALL YOUR HEART, AND WITH ALL YOUR SOUL, AND WITH ALL YOUR MIND.' This is the great and foremost commandment. The second is like it, 'YOU SHALL LOVE YOUR NEIGHBOR AS YOURSELF.'"[3]

Why would we focus all our attention on bringing people into the organization instead of caring for those that are already there? Why would we adopt children into our family if our current children were not being cared for properly? If we are going to keep opting for a centralized church that we say makes effective use of resources, then we should be ever diligent about applying those resources effectively into the nurture and care of the individual. In online communities, I hear it every day. People are finding acceptance, love and healing outside of the organizational church. They feel like they were supporting the organization of the church and the church was not supporting them.

Before you get defensive, I get it! I was a pastor for 20 years and I know that there is never enough time or resources to *minister* to everyone. That is why I think the church as an organization needs a total overhaul and not just a few tweaks. It doesn't at all resemble a family and it is hard to see it as a body.

---

**3** Matthew 22:37–39

I don't think evangelism is the main thing, and here is why. I think when evangelism is the main thing, the church organization becomes more like a sales team than a family or body. When everything is geared toward attracting new members, the main thing gets lost. But, when love is the main thing, then "making disciples" is what naturally happens. Love is really the only thing that changes the world. Early Christians were characterized by their love, not their salesmanship. If the church learns to love the world like God does, the church will not even have an evangelism committee—much less a budget for it!

## *Laura*

Yesterday I got a text message from a friend. She had posted something on Facebook that was definitely meant to help other teachers. It was something that she believed with all her heart. It did just what it was supposed to do: help teachers. She received so much positive feedback, but also noticed some negative comments attached to her post. In all the amazing, glowing compliments, what she focused on were the couple of negative comments. She was distraught. In my response to her heart-broken text to me, I wanted to assure her to "keep the main thing the main thing." It's funny that those words came out in a text and then Karl said that would be the title of our first chapter of this book.

When I told her, "Keep the main thing the main thing," I was not referring to anything church or religious related. For me, keeping the main thing the main thing is all about staying true to who you are. Being a pastor's wife for 20 years, it was not inside the walls of the church where I learned this—or maybe it was. As a pastor's wife, I knew the main thing to be one of two things: First, Jesus. Nothing was supposed to come before Jesus. Second, keeping up appearances as the dutiful wife and mother. I mean, what would people think about me if my kids weren't perfect, and my husband wasn't 100% supported despite my own voice and desires? Now, before I go any further, the expectation of being a dutiful wife and mother did NOT come from Karl. It came from the pressures of living in a fishbowl. Everything I did or did not do would be scrutinized by the church and the small towns we served.

Here is what I have learned since leaving church and the message I was trying to get across to my friend: We need to keep the main thing the main thing and, for me, that means living as my *authentic self.* That means not letting the crowd, be it a group of teachers or a church congregation, tell me who I am or who I should be. It is about finding people who will allow me to explore my authentic self and show others abundant grace in my search.

For me, those people are my family: my husband Karl, my son Jordan, and my daughters Abbey and Lily. They surround me with a never ending stream of grace to not only find who I am, but to completely be who I am at the moment. They encourage me to explore and grow and decide for myself, even when it's scary.

This means that I surround myself with love and courage to grow into the best version of myself. Becoming the best version of myself, I am able to love those around me in an *authentic* way that has the power to shape the world.

So, for me, being authentic is keeping the main thing, the main thing. And, if church forces me away from living authentically, then why should I go?

# 2

# ADDICTED TO CHURCH

*"Religion is the opium of the people."* [4]

KARL MARX

## *Karl*

Recently, we interviewed Cindy Wang Brandt on our podcast, *The Desert Sanctuary.* Don't blame her for anything I say, but her suggestion inspired this thought process. She stressed that everyone should take a "gap year off" from church which she felt would help people gain perspective and heal if necessary.[5] Although I agree with this now, I couldn't have imagined that for the past 25 years. This got me thinking about why I had never fancied this before now. I had a tough time even taking a week off, or not going to church while on vacation.

Could it be that I was addicted to religion and/or church?

---

**4** https://law.marquette.edu/facultyblog/2015/01/karl-marx-on-religion/

**5** Cindy Wang Brandt from episode 50 of The Desert Sanctuary Podcast

Some of our ministry to smaller churches brought us into contact with addicts and former addicts. I noticed that those who were able to leave their addictions often developed dependencies in other areas of their life. I am now considering the idea that maybe most of us at least have a low-grade addiction to several things in our lives. For some of us, it is work. For others, it is food. Still others, it is the appreciation and praise of others. Church and religion may not be the *worst* of our addictions, but they still seem like addictions to me.

But isn't church really designed to be addictive? Think about it. At the typical seeker-sensitive church, someone greets you at the door, smiles at you, looks you in the eye and shakes your hand. This is terribly effective at making you feel welcome and valuable. You are "ushered" into a comfortable environment where soft music is usually playing. To me, church always smells good as well. I don't know if it's true, but it seems that way. I call the service the "show." I don't see it as a derogatory term (I like going to shows), but it is a show. There are parts to play, it's rehearsed, and it is orchestrated and designed to elicit a response. The sermon is prepared and usually involves a problem that is resolved in about 25 minutes.

The typical service at a normal church is ordered, pleasant, often exciting and moving, and usually evokes some type of positive feeling. Many times, there is some positive change to our attitude and the way we approach life. But anything that alters our mood can also become addictive. It's not wrong that we get excited, or cry, or even become sad. But it is problematic when the feelings and emotions don't last, and we have to return week-after-week to *recharge*. Often, religious people try to satisfy their addiction with doing more or obsessing over trying to do it better.

Religious addicts become preoccupied with their rituals, and their mood alters when they behave religiously. Dale S. Ryan and Jeff

VanVonderen talk about religious addiction in their article, *When Religion Goes Bad.*[6] They explain that usually on Monday, when our mood alters downward, we become *preoccupied* with the thing that made us feel good. We go through ritualization or "pre-using" until we get the chance to *use* again. After a sermon, church members have repeatedly thanked me for giving them their "fix." They often say, "I *needed* that," and complained of how that feeling most often didn't last past their first day back to work. I would estimate that most of us who are religious are addicts to one degree or another. Ryan and VanVonderen say, "Anything that alters our mood can become addictive."

"Hi, I'm Karl and I'm a churchaholic"

I have said to multiple people, "I really, really miss preaching." I could give you many reasons for this, but the biggest reason is because it's a rush. Writing, to some degree, has elements of the same "fix." When the thoughts come together and then when people respond, there is a rush of positive feeling that subsides when enough people criticize the work or even just when a little time passes. Thus, the addiction. I need to write something or preach or something! I need a fix!

I'm not trying to convince people to stop going to church, or stop writing or preaching, or anything like that. Human beings have been finding ways to do religion since, well, since forever. We don't need to eliminate sugary sweet food from the world, we just can't get our sustenance from it. If we do, we're going to become addicts. Instead, we need to find something deeper—something less mood altering and more heart-nurturing.

---

**6** https://www.spiritualabuse.com/?page_id=46

I talked to a couple of contemplative people last week. When they talked about their practices, they talked about them like the practices actually sustained them. They loved their practices, but they didn't seem to be addicted to them. Instead, they even talked about setting practices aside for a time to try a new practice or even just to take some time off. There seemed to be less of a roller coaster ride and more of a peaceful journey. They felt free to select the practice that served them, or even to not do anything if that was best for them at the time.

These days, I have lost the addiction to emotional church services. I prefer practices that touch my heart and truly sustain me. Mindfulness and contemplative practices seem more like solid food to me, and I often don't have to *do* anything to find the peace I need. Sometimes just being *where I am* and *who I am* is enough.

My son was a pastor's kid most of his life. Much of his childhood was spent in the sound booth. He was my sound guy for many years. When he wrote a chapter in my first book, he talked about some of the ridiculous things he saw in church. To be fair, he also talked about the things he didn't like at school. He was probably the first in our family to call the church service "the show." This kind of broke my heart, but I'm actually glad he didn't become addicted to religion or church. Instead, he found some good practices and developed into a tremendous human being in his own right.

I pray that you never become addicted to anything (Not food, not work, and not religion). I hope you find the right practices that will sustain you. Then, you will not be dependent on an organization to provide you anything.

## *Laura*

I have always been a creature of habit. I am very routine oriented and when I get out of my routine, I experience a very visceral response. You could say that I struggle to get outside of my comfort zone. I find routine to be a very safe and comforting thing in my life. It was also a wonderful thing when raising babies. If they got their naps at the same time every day, they were typically happy babies, and therefore, I was a happy mamma!

When something unexpected happened, however, I didn't handle the change very well. I guess you could say I was "addicted" to my routine. Now, let me preface this by saying there is nothing inherently wrong with a schedule or routine; without it there would be chaos. I do not thrive in chaos, not even a little!

Church was always part of my routine. Every Sunday there was Sunday school and church, and every Wednesday there was church and youth group. Let's not forget the summer church ritual of Vacation Bible School. None of these activities are "wrong" or "bad." There was, however, a feeling of "have to" associated with these activities. To this day, I cannot tell you why I participated in them or literally made my children participate in them, except to tell you that it was an expected part of my routine, and, truth be told, it was my duty as a pastor's wife. To not participate never seemed like an option to me.

Even during the interview process at each church, I was asked what I could contribute to the church and its activities. While I was honest and straight up told them I don't play the piano or organ and I don't want to be responsible for the nursery, there were still expectations. While at that moment, the Search Committee seemed to understand my position; once in the thick of ministry, if I was not participating, the emotional repercussions were sometimes harsh.

I did get things out of these events. I think my children did as well, to some degree. However, for me personally, it was an *addiction to the routine of church activities* more than a love for them or even a love for God that was the central theme! In fact, when I couldn't go to church or a church activity for some reason—and it had to be a good reason—I experienced guilt and shame. I had to explain why I wasn't there. I felt not only were people in the congregation questioning my whereabouts, but the God I served was also unhappy with me for "skipping." Feelings of guilt and shame are hardly reasons to participate in church but are often what draw us back in when we pull away.

Today I am still very routine oriented. I wake up every day at the same time and go through the same routine to get ready for work. I take the same route every day. I love the fact that my schedule at school is consistent. There is truly something "safe" about having a routine. However, church and church activities are no longer routine in my life. And, for the first time in what seems like forever, I have no guilt or shame associated with not going to church. I had to leave. I had to break that addictive part of my routine because it was toxic to my soul.

3

# THE SERVICES OF THE CHURCH

## *Karl*

Imagine you are in the 1930's, or maybe even the 1950's. During those decades there were a lot of smaller towns and more small-town churches where people came together as a community. There was usually a guy that had some religious training who came and addressed the congregation. At that time, it was probably much needed instruction and encouragement.

Do we still need this *sermon*, or more specifically, do we need it to be at the building? I can watch my five favorite pastors and their most recent sermon without leaving my house on Sunday morning. In addition, I drive an hour to and from work—that didn't happen in the 50's and I usually listen to a podcast, sermon, or speech going to and from work. I average probably 10-12 hours of sermons/podcasts/documentaries each week and then I come to church on Sunday to hear the "message."

When Jesus told his followers to make more disciples (learners), the American church took that to heart. I have always said one of the functions of the church is *discipleship*, which usually means instruction or learning. I understand that it could mean much more than that, but this also leaves me with a similar question: *why do we need to come to a specific place to be discipled?* To be honest, I have experienced some tremendous growth over the past two years via the internet and groups that I'm associated with online. I've read dozens of books by people I respect. Being outside the church for a time, I now wonder why I need to go *there* to *learn*.

Think about it for a moment. 1,500 members get up on Sunday morning and get dressed, then many have a fight on the way out the driveway, then they drive to a specific building that may be a fair distance away. Then each of them gets out of their cars and go into the building, possibly have coffee there, then they listen to someone instruct them how to be a better Christian. In the 21st century, this seems ridiculous to me now.

But what about small groups?

The small group experience that seems to help us so much in this area is so often available online. At church, I have to wait for the right classes to be offered (if they are ever offered), but at home, I can pick out what I want to learn, discuss it in an online group, and even watch videos on demand to help reinforce and solidify what I've learned. I may just be lucky, but I find a lot of wise people online. And is it just me or are the same 20 to 30 people always in the discipleship classes? For teaching purposes, Jesus brought people together; I have to imagine if he had YouTube and Facebook and Print-on-Demand, he might have done some things differently. There is certainly a place for face-to-face teaching, but we have so many options today.

When I ask people about *worship* experiences, they usually describe a time out in nature or a time when they are alone or oddly enough when they are driving. I agree there is something about live music and corporate worship. So, I'm willing to concede that it has its place, and it has some value. But how many people have to be there before its corporate and do you have to have a "corporation" (organization) to consider it corporate worship? Couldn't it be much simpler than that and not cost nearly as much? If I'm watching the Avett Brothers on stage, it's a little better than listening on YouTube, but increasingly I would rather worship in solitude or with a few friends. That could just be me.

Lately, I've been questioning whether God really even desires worship. To me, that is kind of like my boss giving me a job and accepting me into the organization, then demanding that I praise him every day for hiring me instead of just thanking him once. It seemed immature to demand that someone worship you.

And didn't Jesus do away with the sacrificial system and tell the Samaritan woman that, in the future, we wouldn't go to a place to worship. Although he was vague about the meaning of spirit and truth worship, he was pretty clear that we wouldn't be worshiping in a place in the future. And the future is now!

Since I recently decided to take a break from church, the one thing I have missed already is the *fellowship* with certain people, but I do have a HeartConnexion group that I connect with occasionally. This is a group that I had an immersive, healing experience with. We meet only occasionally with a few of the members and support each other online. I have several groups online that I interact with, sometimes daily. We debate, discuss, console, and encourage each other. It is surprisingly helpful in a lot of ways. We have a new contemplative group that is extremely helpful to me.

Occasionally, I do gatherings at the house for assorted reasons. Laura and I fellowship daily, and we have family that we talk to at various intervals. This doesn't even include work, and all the other people I have contact with every day. I am kind of introverted, but I don't think I'm deprived in any way. Occasionally, I schedule time with my spiritual director or have lunch to catch up with a friend, but I don't see the need for an organization to manage my fellowship.

For simplicity's sake, let's just agree that *evangelism*, if that's even a real thing, really happens outside the church and it should happen more organically. Like many things, we have changed it into something it was probably never intended to be, so I'm not willing to even waste much energy on it right now. You can't really have altar calls at home or in the coffee shop, but someone tried it on a podcast I was on the other day. Since I discussed evangelism earlier in this book, I'll leave it alone for now.

I really enjoyed *communion* at the last church I attended, but was it really a ceremony originally? I'm not sure about this one. I have always thought that it was more about people coming together. I love the "open table" sentiment where all are welcome, but that is also an attitude and a lifestyle. My friend, Steve Daugherty, stressed that when Jesus said, "Do This," he was talking about the coming together as much as the eating and drinking.[7] I don't know for sure, but I think it could happen anywhere!

By the way, if I could change worship, I would use the word communion in its place. It seems important to me to commune with God, but the meaning of that phrase is also changing.

As they say, "things change." Jesus told us as much when he told the woman that people would eventually worship in "spirit and truth."[8]

---

7 Daughtery, Steve, *Experiments in Honesty: Meditations on Love, Fear and the Honest to God Naked Truth*. Nashville: Worthy Publishing, 2018, 81

**8** John 4:24

We know the temple building was not what God had in mind. His idea was that His temple was to be inside of us. I'm not questioning the presence of the church in this age; I'm just questioning the location and method. How much money could we put to better use? Probably a lot!

I resist the urge to go back to the first century model. I assume there are lessons to learn in examining *how* they did it. There are often great lessons to learn in orthodoxy and orthopraxy, but we shouldn't get too tangled up in either one. God is still the same, but the times we live in are extremely different. For one thing, I can access a vast majority of the information on the planet without leaving my easy chair. We must start by admitting that this changes a lot of how we do things just like the printing press changed a lot of things five hundred years ago. I can drive the distance that Mary and Joseph walked to Bethlehem in just over an hour simply to have a meal or pick up something at our favorite grocery store.

I remember watching Star Trek and marveling at the communicators that didn't have a cord and thinking that would be so cool, but it will never happen. That "flip phone" type of communicator is what I make fun of the guy at work for carrying because it's "ancient" now. Phasers were considered other-worldly, but we now just call them lasers—pretty basic and about as common as a medical scanner, which they also had on Star Trek. There is often some value to "going back" and rediscovering the past, but often we get stuck there and don't embrace the possibilities for the future.

What if I could do everything the organizational church does for no additional tax (tithe)? What if I could check just as many boxes and even find something a little deeper without professional clergy and an organization looking over my shoulder? What if we could redirect all of those resources into effective ministry instead of spending 70% of all that money on salaries and buildings?

I think we can!

Maybe we couldn't do that 100 years ago. Maybe we couldn't even have done it 30 years ago. But I think we can now! The people that have the most to lose (livelihood) are the ones that have to consider this, otherwise we will just start shaming and blaming and talking about things that really aren't the issue.

When our only option was the horse and buggy, it didn't make sense to move off the family farm, so very few people did. When air travel and reliable automobiles became an option, it was more realistic to travel all over the world. In a comparable way, when people worked 16 hours a day and had no other options for the things we get from "church," it made sense to go to a specific place at a specific time to get those things. But now we have better options.

I don't know if I'll ever attend a church in a building again. If I do, it will be less centralized and more personal. I really can't imagine going to a building or paying a person to supervise my spiritual life ever again. I want my practices to be more contemplative and way more practical. I already left traditional ministry because thinking like this makes it hard to fit into a traditional model, even if it is progressive. I pray for my other pastor friends that are making courageous moves to live more authentic lives. I also admire the ones that must stay where they are for now.

I don't want to go back to the 1950's or the first century. I want to live in the decade I find myself in with as much wisdom and sensibility as I can muster. Just like Jesus challenged the status quo of his time, I want to speak up against things that aren't working. Let us at least consider what change could look like even if it means we must change dramatically.

## *Laura*

I think I have had a "love/hate" relationship with church most of my life. Church was something I did—it was part of our Sunday routine. I don't believe there is anything inherently wrong with church being part of a family's schedule. Isn't that how we are taught to raise our children? We bring them to church and there they find God and the people who also love God—their community. Honestly, that is how we raised our children. They never professed a desire to attend or not to attend. It was just something that has always been expected. When Karl was called into the ministry, it then became mandatory. The strange thing is, the more I tried to embrace the aspects of the church service, the more I began to question its purpose.

I am a self-diagnosed creature of habit. I am very routine driven. I wake up at the same time every morning and my routine for getting ready for work is the same every day. It's pretty ridiculous, but there is a certain amount of security I get in keeping a very tight routine. With that in mind, you would think I'd love the routine of the American church service. I admit, the pageantry of many modern-day churches does tap into my emotional side. I have found true worship and truth spoken in all the churches we have either pastored or attended. However, as I have gone further into my deconstruction, the pageantry begins to fall flat. The routine of the service is what has now become too predictable.

I believe my deconstruction has brought on so many challenging questions—some probably less than popular for the average church. And, most church services cater to new members, so keeping the service routine the same is most likely on purpose and essential to modern churches.

So, that begs the question, *why not get involved in some church programs?* That's a great and valid question. Today's churches do have several programs, from adult Sunday School classes to Wednesday night Bible studies, and beyond. All these programs are a wonderful way to interact with a church community and learn more about Jesus, however, typically these programs are very denominationally based. What I mean by that is they are going to center around that denomination's beliefs and teachings. For example, Karl pastored a couple of Baptist churches. Their literature came from only a couple of Baptist approved sources. With this method, there is little to no room for questioning. Perhaps a bolder person wouldn't care, but part of my story is losing my voice, which I'll talk more about later. So, for me to have the courage to stand up and question the teachings of a church program just wasn't going to happen. Besides, how would it look if the pastor's wife were questioning the very doctrine of the church her husband was pastoring?

Finally, let's talk about my third aspect of the church service, which is *people.* Karl likes to say that I make friends wherever I go. I really do love people! I still have a treasured friend, Jill, from the very first church we pastored in Stella, Nebraska. That was over 20 years ago! A community of people is a gift. As a pastor's wife, it can be a little tricky when it comes to finding your tribe in a church. In my experience, at first, everyone wants to be your best friend. In fact, I distinctly remember one woman at the last church we pastored telling me I was her "best friend" after only knowing me for a couple of weeks. I remember thinking that was extremely strange because we barely knew each other. For the most part, however, I appreciated how welcoming people were when we came to pastor a church or when we visited various churches over the years.

While I am sure part of this friendliness is an effort to attract new members, or being incredibly thankful, we were there to save a dying church. It is a wonderful feeling to be wanted and welcomed. Who doesn't want to feel like they "belong?" However, our experience doesn't end there. Unfortunately, as time went on, the true nature of the people we were serving began to show. Truthfully, most, if not all, people have an agenda and church people are no exception. While members were grateful at first that we had come to resurrect a dying church, as things began to improve, and the more Karl shared his heart and vision, the more fear and stubbornness we began to see in the same people who were warm and welcoming only a few short years or months ago.

While people want change, their toleration for it can only go so far before they feel uncomfortable and scared. In those moments, fear can show itself in very ugly ways. Heels dig in very deep and all the things we were once praised for now came into question. Doing things, the way they have always done them becomes a form of twisted security, even though those ways nearly shut the church's doors.

For me personally, the church service became a game I couldn't play any longer. I find I don't need the pageantry. Where I once craved the church service for the emotional rush, I now find that in my morning routine. I am an early riser as I said previously, so being alone with myself to set my intentions for the day truly does center me and brings me, not an emotional rush that over time diminishes and requires "more," but emotional stability for my soul. In regard to programming, I get so much from the various podcasts that I listen to on a daily basis. My podcast lists are places where questions and doubts are welcome. I feel challenged. They are places where I have totally dismantled the God, I thought I knew. But in these places, I have been able to be incredibly angry and it was okay. This format allows me to be a true seeker of the Divine without having to conform to what is already established.

I have also been able to connect with some truly inspirational and grace-filled people via podcasts. The beauty of where I am now is that I don't believe that the only way I can find anything of spiritual value for my life is inside the church walls. There is so much pageantry, programming, and people outside of its walls as well. We simply need to be open to what is all around us.

The God I have served all of my life is not real, but the only place I can truly see the Divine is outside of the walls of church. This Divine source is not confined. They are not just in the worship songs or the hymns. They are not just in the activities or the programs. The Divine is so much more and cannot be contained. They are there every day. They are in my routine and outside of it. They are present on a Sunday morning breakfast date with my husband, or they are with me listening to Christmas music as I write this chapter. Wherever I am, whatever I am doing, they are because I am.

4

# THE COST OF DOING BUSINESS

## *Karl*

Recently, I became curious about what it takes to run a church. Although I managed a church budget for almost 20 years at three different small churches, I couldn't remember any of the amounts that I was trying to recall, so I did a little searching (I wouldn't call it research). Here are some rough numbers:

*What does a church receive in offerings?* Depending on the type of church, annual giving seems to be somewhere between $800 and $1,400 a year per person.[9] Most of the church members don't tithe or give anything, but that is the average. For simplicity, let's just say that is $1000 per year per person. So, if you took one of the Facebook groups I am involved with (around 1,100 people) and formed a

---

**9** https://www.vancopayments.com/egiving/blog/average-church-giving-statistics

church, the income for that organization would be about $1.1 million a year based on the above average.

*Where does the money go?* Sounds like a question we would ask of the government, but it's a fair question. What do we get back for that money? On average, churches spend about 47% of the money they receive to compensate their staff.[10] This includes salaries and other reimbursements like housing allowances and mileage reimbursement. My main concern with staff is just a nagging little thought: are they spending most of their time doing ministry or running the organization? I know they all have good hearts and work hard, but what percentage of that work would go away if there was no organization? Twenty-two percent of church income goes to property and maintenance, and 10% helps keep programs running. Of the remaining budget, 5 to 10% goes to mission type expenses.[11]

So, for our fictitious Facebook church, do these 1,100 people really need to spend $1.1 Million to pay staff, maintain a building, and sustain the programs that make it viable? I suppose that is a question all 1,100 people must answer for themselves. With access to information and online connection abilities, do we really need to do this, or do it in the same manner we have always done it?

What if the headquarters were much smaller and simply a place to equip people with supplies to do ministry and counsel and train others? In the Christian faith, the apostle Paul seemed to think that a pastor's job is to equip the people to do ministry. If that ministry is really done outside the walls of the church building, couldn't the

---

**10** https://www.pnwumc.org/news/how-churches-spend-their-money/

**11** https://www.churchlawandtax.com/web/2019/march/how-churches-spend-money.html

space for the leaders be a much smaller office space? Here, occasional equipping type classes and essential meeting and administrative work could be done on a less than full time basis.

For that matter, what if a much smaller *staff* recorded classes and online resources that supported people's learning from their remote locations? Even a church of 1,100 usually doesn't need to house people for education all at the same time. Training is usually for an hour on Sunday and a couple of hours on another night. If the staff didn't need to maintain a large building, it would require much less of everything, including building maintenance, staff, bookkeepers, less programming, etc.

What if the organization just rented a meeting place occasionally—like once a quarter—for *gatherings*, fellowship, and to celebrate? As I mentioned in a previous chapter, with advances in technology and the way people get information, the need for gathering together to receive the sermon, experience worship, and get coffee could most definitely be done from a distance. Occasionally, they could rent a space and come together; but it doesn't have to be a continual thing. If a couple rents the church to get married, they could just as easily rent another facility.

What if people maximized the places where they are already going to *fellowship* and get together with other people, instead of coming to a specific location at a specific time to be supervised in their gathering? I don't have anything against large group gatherings, but it seems to make fellowship tougher for some people, not easier. I recently went to a somewhat larger church, but noticed I mainly interacted with the same 8 to 10 people every week. I was glad to see them, but I wondered why I couldn't meet them somewhere else. As an introvert, I would much rather meet someone at a coffee shop where we can talk, than go to a huge building that has a coffee shop in it along with

1,100 other people. It's hard enough to talk to 2 or 3 people at once, let alone much more than that.

What if half of the budget were spent on *social justice* issues? What could we do with $550,000 a year in our little Facebook church? I couldn't find a consistent number on total giving for all church organizations. But let's just say it's $50 Billion. If that is true, what could we do nationwide with $25 Billion going directly to the poor and homeless and other charity groups? When the church was small and met in homes, it was particularly good at sharing its resources. Now, most of that money goes to running the organization.

I know some churches do better than others in some of these areas. For example, some churches give more to outside charities. Some have less staff than average, but some also have more.

The small churches that I pastored had relatively small budgets. Attendance was usually under one hundred, so the budget was less than $100,000. Most of the congregation was closer to that original mindset of the early church and was good at sharing resources, and they were usually pretty thrifty and expected me to follow suit. But that didn't mean we didn't follow the same models, financially. About half of the "income" still went to the staff (me), and about 20% to the cost of maintaining the building. We spent a fair amount of time maintaining the organization and holding meetings. We still practiced for the "show," and worked toward that happening each week.

Even if we don't cut the staff in half and move into a much smaller building, I wish we could examine it in a realistic way. I don't think future generations will be able to comprehend why we spent so much money to gather in one place when we could do it in a better, more efficient way. I don't think they will understand why we need such a big organization when we can do much of it ourselves.

## *Laura*

As I write this, it is the Christmas season. I love watching Christmas cookie and cake challenges on the Food Network. In between programming there are the commercials that we are accustomed to seeing. The interesting thing is at this most "wonderful time of the year," we seem to be inundated with commercials petitioning us to give to various charitable causes such as mental health, homelessness, and domestic abuse, just to name a few.

In years past, I never gave a second thought to seeing these commercials, since I was giving money to our church and the organization was supposed to handle those kinds of things. Since we stopped going to church, these commercials have started hitting me harder, and I have been questioning why these issues are so prevalent in one of the greatest, richest countries. Then, when I think of all of our mega churches that have millions in their budgets, I wonder why we are not addressing the issues like mental health, homelessness, and domestic abuse.

Churches usually find ways to minister to the communities around them, but as with any budget, only so much can be allocated to reaching real needs of the community. Much of what the church does to reach out to our communities are Sunday school, Vacation Bible School, various seasonal activities such as Trunk or Treat, and special services such as Christmas Eve. While these draw people, I wonder if they are truly meeting the needs of all those who were once outside our church with genuine issues and real hurts, who are now on the inside. Those issues don't just disappear once they enter the doors of the church.

To be fair, we have been a part of churches that have weekly outreach activities, such as *Celebrate Recovery* to help those who are recovering addicts. There are, however, so many additional issues that the church can never possibly mitigate and keep the doors of the organization open at the same time. While it may seem like I am picking on bigger churches, the same can be said for small, rural churches of which Karl and I have pastored for twenty years. As we know with our personal budgets, we can't do everything.

Since leaving church, my perspective of the church has shifted. I am no longer convinced that we need a physical church building to do the work of the church. As far as we know, Jesus didn't have board meetings, goal setting sessions, and budgets. Instead, He spent most of his time doing and being with those in need (spiritually, emotionally, and physically). The amount of money it takes to keep a church staff, utilities, and programs going could possibly be used to actually reach people like Jesus did. Are church budgets too large? You be the judge. Could the money for church staff and activities be better utilized by giving to the many needs of people? I think so.

I wish I had all the answers. Here is what I do know: sometimes the cost of doing the business of the church truly does cost us. It cost me the freedom to love people unconditionally. It pushed me towards associating with people that were more like me even though that was not its intent. Since leaving the church, I am finding freedom in being with and for people. I am learning things outside the church that I wasn't receiving inside the church, including the churches we pastored. Now that I am outside of the constraints of a church denomination, I see and love all people differently. I am not afraid to speak up for those that live in silence and in the margins.

Since deconstructing, I am learning that saying Jesus loves everyone means *every one*. They do not have to be a certain denomination. They don't have to live a certain lifestyle. They don't have to make a certain amount of money. They don't have to look, speak, or act anything like me. I found it essential to get outside the business and the busyness of the church and go, like Jesus, and simply be present with people. No agenda. No budget. No programs. Just being.

# 5

# WE CAN DO BETTER

## *Karl*

I never really liked "Devil's Advocates" when I was a pastor. Over time, in business, I learned to value those that asked the tough questions. I'm really not trying to be critical in this book, I simply want to start some discussion that might help churches and individuals make some progress. When I was a pastor, most clergy gave the almost automatic response, "Well you know, Karl, no church is perfect and certainly not ours." I know from experience that this is a deflection that really means, *I don't have time to even consider that right now–I have more than enough irons in the fire.* Let me just stress the stakes are high and time is running short! But I guess that's what Devil's advocates always say.

I have repeatedly stated that I admire those that would preserve the local church, but progress requires honesty. We should not only discover where we are going (goal setting, vision, mission), but we should also accurately articulate where we have fallen short in the past. We need to talk openly about what we have not done well. We need to admit our failures if we're going to have success in the future.

In many ways, churches have often been considered *sanctuaries.* In some cases, it has been literal—in other cases spiritual or figurative. I would suggest the American church has become anything but a sanctuary for some people. It is not a safe place for many. The scandals in the various churches where children have been molested is widespread, but it also raises the obvious question, "If those are the ones that we know about, then how many more are there that didn't say anything?" Our churches are too segregated, non-affirming, and judgmental. After being a pastor for 20 years, I left church life feeling like it was the last place I would want to be vulnerable or go to feel safe. It simply didn't live up to the hype, and in many ways, failed to make me feel secure.

Sarah Bessey got me thinking the other day, while listening to a sermon she preached in 2016. She was explaining why she couldn't attend church at that time. She said, "The church didn't have room for my grief." There is a certain commitment to happiness and joy in the typical American church. We can't admit we're not doing well and it's not okay to not be okay. In a contemplative group we started recently, I instructed the people not to do any side talking when someone shared. The reason for this is so that people won't try to fix each other. Someone that is struggling makes us incredibly uncomfortable and we don't allow them just to be sad, angry, confused, or depressed. We want to get through this quickly so we can all be "happy" again.

When I propose that maybe we could do church somewhere else besides a dedicated building, the first thing that people (especially pastors) suggest is that we need a community. They say it in many different ways, but that's what they mean. "We have a deep need for community!" I agree, I would just submit that the typical church in America is not particularly good at community. We may be good at giving people casseroles when someone dies, but how often are we vulnerable at church? How many of our deepest secrets do we share with the congregation? For that matter, how much time do we spend with the people we worship with? I'm sure there are exceptions, but in general, I would have a tough time characterizing what we do in the typical church with the word community.

This point is sure to cause consternation, but here goes. For years, we have been arguing over hymns and choruses—contemporary or traditional. All the while, the culture has been moving to more contemplative and ascetic practices. The most shocking thing I did as a pastor was to admit that I did meditation and yoga. Our worship doesn't work *at all* for people like cultural creatives, some introverts, and those that desire more contemplative types of practices. The church has always been slow in relating to its culture because it always claims to be authentic, which often begs the question "what are we being true to?" It is usually just the practices of the near past, and nothing else.

Even with the Great Commission, we often get it wrong. We imagine disciple-making as instructional, instead of something more cathartic and organic. Excessive questions are discouraged, and we generally try to keep classes and instruction limited to things that are easily explained. We make it as efficient as we can, while most of us secretly long for something deeper and more heart centered.

As a pastor, I remember being frustrated when I tried to deal with sexual addiction in the church. The Church in America historically has not been effective at mental health and other difficult issues. We generally rely on spiritual bypassing and assume God will just miraculously zap away the problems we have. When people don't get better, they injure each other. Hurt people, hurt people. It's kind of a cycle. It might even be an epidemic. Before we shame someone back to church, we might want to consider that there may be a real, painful reason people are not coming.

I hope this doesn't sound like I'm being too critical. I'm really trying to ask the question, "How can we do better?" I don't want to stay out of church, but until one or both of us gets better, we can't be together. I wish I were joking! I don't hate the church; I'm just trying to imagine a better future for both of us.

## *Laura*

Most of my life I have been known as a "peace-keeper." I'm not sure if it is because I am the middle child, an Enneagram 9, or a combination of the two. I am typically the one people come to when there is strife. I just look, and perhaps behave, like a mediator.

There is something selfless about being a "peace-keeper." You are always available to help those in need, no matter who, where, or when. So, when I became a pastor's wife, the peacemaker part of me fell quickly and quietly into that role. The problem was, who was I supposed to go to when I needed someone to talk to or help me when I had a crisis? As a pastor's wife, I honestly could not go to anyone inside the church. In my experience, the church "prayer chain" is often a cover for gossip. You know what I mean, someone relays a prayer request, but every time you call the next person, they want a little more information so they can pass that onto the next person. Sometimes, even if there was no additional information given, when the next person was called and questions were asked, assumptions were given out freely. Those assumptions were then passed down the prayer chain.

Maybe you think I could have gone to my mom or my sisters. I definitely could have, and I did on occasion, but here is the problem with that: I am part of their family. They would automatically come to my defense and even want to fight against the church for me. I also dealt with the guilt of possibly turning them away from the church. So, maybe I could talk to Karl? If I talked to Karl and truly shared all the doubts and questions I had, I ran the risk of destroying his ministry. I could not be responsible for that.

To be fair, Karl never knew of my struggles, and I don't think he would have ever held me responsible for "destroying" his ministry. The spiritual trauma I was struggling with, however, had me thinking completely differently. So, maybe I could just reach out to people I knew outside the church. Again, while I tried, people couldn't really understand because they were of another denomination or simply because being a pastor's wife is in a league of its own!

To cope with this dilemma, I became incredibly good at playing the games of church. I was silencing my voice and spiritually bypassing everyone, including myself. Spiritual bypassing is the process of saying very spiritual things in order to placate how someone is really feeling. For example, someone comes to us with a very real hurt, and we say things like, "God is in control," or "Just pray about it," or "I'll pray for you," or "I'm sure it will work out." Spiritual bypassing is putting a Band-Aid over people's hurts instead of validating them. I get that they have programs to help people deal with grief, but that must be done at a certain time, and only when they offer it.

The truth is, people can't compartmentalize their grief, and it can't be "fixed" in an hour once a week. When people spiritually bypass someone who has already been traumatized by the church, it only adds more trauma because it sends wrong messages like, "Obviously I don't have enough faith, or I would know God is in control. If I were a good Christian, I would be able to pray through this." Or even worse, "I shouldn't be feeling this."

So, how can we do better? True healing comes with people who will sit in it with us, and when I say sit, I mean sit. Not talk. Not try to fix it. Sit with us and speak truth to our soul in that moment. Let us know that "this sucks!" That includes people in the church. The church would do better to be there, and sit, and be with people in their grief, not at a scheduled time of the week, but whenever. That is probably a tall order. Therefore, if that can't be accomplished in the organization of the church, I think one way we can do better is to make room for grief in our church communities. We can let people know that it is ok to not be ok. That there is nothing wrong with you when you are in struggle. God does not love you any less because of your struggle. It's ok not to know what or how to pray. That doesn't change how God sees you.

For me to heal (truly heal), I have had to take a step back from the church. I have found that, for now, I cannot heal within organized religion. The strange thing is leaving church has brought me peace. My world didn't fall apart. In fact, some things started to come together, and I am seeing the Divine in a new way. Nothing seems rushed. I have permission to seek, to question, and most personally important, to sit with myself and find my own peace. Perhaps this is a more authentic revelation of my truth as a "peacemaker."

# 6

# WOULD JESUS GO TO CHURCH?

## *Karl*

When we decided not to go to church anymore, we didn't really know whether it was a permanent decision or just what we would be doing for a time. It probably depends upon which one of us you talk to and what day it is. One thing is for sure, we need some time to heal up from being in church consistently for about 25 years.

The pain is real; it doesn't matter that there are problems in every church. It does matter that, since we left church, we've felt more shaming than actual concern for us. We are not imagining things, it's painful!

Recently, we went to a cafe in Auburn, Nebraska for brunch on Sunday. We had a nice, casual discussion. We really didn't think about church much at all. I have personally experienced a gradual relaxation coming over me the longer we have been "skipping" church.

The only exception was that I was accused of bashing the church when I tried to discuss some of these things openly on Facebook. One fella thought I was trying to get attention. If he only knew how wrong he was about that. What I long for is for the church to address itself to the 21st century and figure out how we can actually help people that have been injured by life, and also by the church.

I am thankful that, along with the challenging situations, we have also experienced some very encouraging and life-giving situations like we did on this recent Sunday.

This little cafe was terribly busy! The other options in town are pizza, Mexican, Chinese and barbecue (not particularly good brunch options). This place was well equipped and smelled like breakfast. I ordered pancakes and breakfast potatoes and anticipated their arrival. About that time, I noticed a guy that looked a little like Santa Claus. He introduced himself to a couple of people and then sat down with another couple. It made me think of the books where John the Apostle, or even Jesus himself, makes an appearance in modern day America and teaches some valuable lessons to an unsuspecting malcontent.

As I mentioned, I have been having discussions online about church this week and reading a book called *Pagan Christianity*, by Frank Viola and George Barna, which shows how many of our traditions are most likely adapted from pagan rituals. Because I posted this online, it kind of inflamed the church goers, especially the ones that live near me, because they assumed it was about them.

Let me just be clear: this is not a direct criticism of any specific church. If the church is working for you, keep doing it. But recognize that it's not working for everyone and try to understand that I would simply like to have some discussions to see if we can somehow become better at doing "church." Even more than that, I want to somehow stop injuring people and help those that are already injured get better.

*So, let's just cut to the chase.*

I don't think Jesus would go to church at all. Even when I was a pastor, when people told the story of a guy walking in the door—you know the one, where people ignore him—then he reveals that He is Jesus. I never bought that story because I just could never picture Jesus walking into a church, at least not like we have it designed. I know he went to the temple because he was raised as a Jew, and that he was occasionally found in Synagogue. But I just could never picture him in a traditional church.

Jesus preferred to do his teaching outdoors. We find him on a boat, on a hillside, in the streets, at a well with an enemy. He was almost never in the same place and seldom on a schedule. On a Sunday morning in Auburn, NE, I could more aptly picture him introducing himself to a table of people and sitting down to eat breakfast with them.

I'm not the right person to ask right now. I'm a little bit raw from allowing myself to get to the point where I could hardly bear to walk in the door of a church. Too much "stuff" without any relief has left me a little short of being bitter and needing to get my bearings. But many of the people I come across these days are feeling the same way. It just doesn't all make sense like it used to.

In her book, *The Great Emergence,* Phyllis Tickle uses the analogy of a "five hundred Year Rummage Sale"[12] to describe how the church tends to "clean house" every five hundred years. The last time this happened was in 1517, about five hundred years ago. The advent and proliferation of the internet is going to lead us to some dramatic changes in how we do church, much like the printing press did at an earlier time.

I don't know all the answers to how it should change, but I know without a doubt that it needs to be reimagined, or it is surely going to

---

**12** Tickle, Phyllis. *The Great Emergence: How Christianity is Changing and Why.* Ada: Baker Books, 2008, 11

fail in the next 10 years. I often ask people, "If you could change the world, what would you change?" Well, if I could change the world, I would change the church.

For all the time we have spent in church, we really should be doing better than we are. Maybe we spent too much time erecting the church building and coming *to* church, when we should have spent time *being* the church. I don't really care whether the church building survives or whether pastors get to keep making money by being pastors. What I care about is that people get better emotionally and learn to live out the Great Commandment to love one another. I don't care if church attendance goes up or down—I want us to be kinder and more compassionate. I don't want to lose another friend because of where I attended or what I believed. I don't want to see another friend burnout as a pastor, or another person get hurt emotionally, because we care too much about the organization of the church and too little about the people in the body of Christ.

I believe we can get better. I want to keep an image of the Santa Claus guy in the café. I will be trying to emulate that guy while my wounds heal. As I build and nurture community, I can love my family and the people I see along the way. I can watch sermons and podcasts and read and pray and meditate. Yesterday, I did a podcast with a couple of my contemplative friends. It was a community, I felt loved, and I learned a couple of things.

For now, these kinds of things are more than good enough for me.

## *Laura*

I wish you could be with Karl and me as we write this book. In many ways it is hilarious because we have quite different writing styles. He seems calm and collected as he writes, cranking out chapter after chapter in about six hours. He has so much knowledge, and he writes from a scholarly and personal perspective. Then there is me. In that six-hour time frame, I get one chapter done! If you could see me, you would see me type two sentences and then put my laptop aside for a five-minute break.

To be fair, watching my holiday cooking shows has me completely distracted! The ironic thing is, I will never make one of those recipes. I'm like a squirrel who sees something shiny! It really does make me chuckle! Unlike Karl, I have no theological training to back me up. My comments and thoughts come strictly from my individual experiences and understanding. So, before I start digging into this chapter, let me be sure I preface it by saying I am going strictly on what the title means to me. So, would Jesus go to church?

My answer to that question is "yes, but." I do believe Jesus would go to church, *but* I believe Jesus would go anywhere people are. I don't think Jesus needs a certain day of the week or an order of worship to simply be present with people. It is important not to put Jesus in a box. The little I know about the Jesus of the Bible, it seems that He was all over the place (much like my writing style). He was in the synagogues, He was at the well, and He was in the desert. He seemed to be wherever people were, but He also took time to be away from people and minister to Himself. This speaks volumes to me, especially as we have personally moved outside of the church walls. Just because we have left the church doesn't mean we have abandoned meeting with people. Church is not the only place where we can encounter others.

In many ways church is where we fellowship with people that are "like" us, which, in my opinion, can be a huge red flag. While there is nothing inherently wrong with being with like-minded people, we can easily become stuck there because it's comfortable. To add to that, most of the people I have encountered inside the church seem to be doing okay. But I also understand that in church we are exceptionally good at spiritually bypassing, so while we appear put together, there are many "walking wounded" inside the church. The catch twenty-two is what was discussed in the previous chapter: there is little to no room or time for grief in the church, so we are inclined to put on a happy face.

I think Jesus would go anywhere to be with people. In fact, maybe He would go to more places outside the church—places where He would find those who truly need Him. I'm not saying church people don't need Jesus, but until we are willing to remove our masks and be authentic, there is only so much Jesus can do inside the walls of the church. I think Jesus would happily stay outside of the church in order to find hearts that are hungry for Him. He goes to great lengths to connect with people. Jesus cannot be contained. Often, we use the church to try to control the Divine by asserting that church is the only place to meet Him (or at least the main place). Also, who says the Divine is a "Him?" Perhaps outside the church we can experience the Divine as so much more.

This morning I listened to Father Richard Rohr's "Christianity and Unknowing" on YouTube[13]. It was just what my heart needed. Father Rohr speaks of how St. Francis saw the Divine in everything, including nature. St. Francis referred to Mother Sky, Brother Fox, and Sister Moon. How beautiful! What an exquisite picture of the Divine that cannot be contained. We find it in everything and everyone around us, inside and outside of the church, in nature and in brick-and-mortar organizations. So, *yes*, perhaps Jesus would probably go to church, *but*

---

**13** https://www.youtube.com/watch?v=MnTC4NNIACk

the Divine cannot be confined to only the church building. They are everywhere we are. Everywhere people are. Everywhere nature is. They are everywhere and I am thankful.

7

# THE THINGS THAT HURT

## *Karl*

We were in the middle of a building program at one of the churches I served. Tensions were a little high because we were all anxious to move forward. We were having church in a double-wide trailer. Often, we would have 50 to 60 people in this hollowed out shell of a building. We raised $40,000 and agreed to move forward on the building program. Someone donated us some land, and we leveled the pad out where we thought it should go and let it settle over the winter. As soon as we could pour a foundation, we were there roughing in plumbing and the work didn't stop, until we moved into the new facility on Easter Sunday. It was quite amazing!

It was over 20 years ago, so I don't remember the timelines very clearly. One thing I do remember is someone calling me over to their house during the process. It's not uncommon as a pastor for this to occur. Someone wants everyone else to do something like they think it should be done so they get aggressive in their persuasiveness. When I took some of this gentleman's statements personally, he calmly exclaimed, "Karl, you need to have thicker skin."

When I explained to him how deeply I loved the people that I served and explained how open my heart was to them, he began to see how his actions and attitudes were hurting me and his eyes began to fill with tears. We just shared a moment and were much better friends afterward, but I realized at that moment that people often expect the pastor to be bulletproof. They also don't realize that even if the shots fired at him bounce off of him, the shrapnel sometimes injures his family.

### A MISUNDERSTANDING

"That's not what I said," I kept repeating in my texts, but she wouldn't listen. Vile, hateful things peppered with accusations kept pouring across my phone. She wouldn't answer the phone and I was beginning to get indications that she was talking to other people. I contacted a couple of people at the Association to let them know we might have a situation.

Laura had become friends with one of the new people at the church. They were "besties" (according to this woman), and our ministry was having an impact on them. I would hug them as they came into church. We personally took them to lunch and spent the Fourth of July watching fireworks with them. They were becoming faithful attenders and we talked about their son helping with worship.

One day, I noticed that the woman was moving slowly from a distance. The next day, I sent a text to ask her if she was feeling okay because I noticed she was moving kind of slow. Obviously, most things are better in person, but I was just trying to express my concern. Did she have a knee problem? I didn't know, so I asked. That is when the electronic world exploded on a Saturday morning, and we experienced our first firestorm at that church.

I later learned that she was probably messaging other people as fast as she was texting me telling them that I had called her "fat." I looked at the text a hundred times; it seemed harmless, but I repeatedly apologized profusely if that was the way she understood it. She was already in full battle mode. I texted her adult son to try to get some clarity. He gave me his opinion, but she soon forbade any of her family to talk to me and threatened me with all kinds of things.

It was just one of the "what the heck?" moments in ministry. I suppose we did some damage control, but several things were for sure: Laura had lost a friend, our ministry took a step back, and we both became a little more cautious with people. We lost a little of our authenticity because we subconsciously felt a need to armor up.

## HE DANCED WITH HIS WIFE

To be fair, there was a little more to it than that. The two issues at hand were tobacco use and dancing. Regardless, he was in my makeshift office, in someone's basement, yelling at me at the top of his lungs. I remained calm for the most part and thanked him for his input, but he was on full tilt, so I just let him tell me why I was unacceptable.

Apparently, it started when he learned that Laura and I were slow dancing at the local street dance. I might add this was an incredibly positive step for the townspeople and some of our members, but this guy believed nothing good could happen at a dance. I knew that he felt this way, but he was not even a member of our church—some of his family was, and I guess, he was protecting them. To be honest, I considered some might not approve, but I didn't know they felt this strongly and I probably would have done it anyway. Just a dance with my wife—you could see that as a positive if you wanted to.

The good side of this story is that we made up later and he changed his approach to some things, but the damage was done. This situation would make me much more cautious and less authentic in the years to come. It also deeply hurt my wife who was just as busy as she could be taking care of our kids and was heartbroken that she couldn't enjoy a night with her husband without being judged. But it wouldn't be the last time someone judged us unfairly.

### THE MINISTRY THAT MIGHT HAVE BEEN

I've always had a heart for people in the margins. Early on, I discovered some of the causes for drug use, homelessness, and other related issues. I developed a compassion for people that were considered "other" by some churches, and we generally had some success ministering to them. So, when I discovered that a man in our association wanted to expand his street ministry to other cities, I invited them to come help us do that where we were. Everything was moving along well, and we had targeted a start date. We would meet in the basement of a bank. All the pieces were falling into place. Then, we had a final meeting with some leaders.

I kept wondering why there were so many people at this meeting. There were extras! It always makes me suspicious when extra people come along to a meeting. Business meetings that are full are almost as suspicious as those that are empty. After we ate, they told me the issue. The lead guy's wife was poking around on Facebook and noticed that my wife and my 21-year-old daughter had gone to have a glass of wine on her 21st birthday. This wife of the preacher had raised a "concern." The meeting ended pleasantly without conflict, but I knew in my heart this ministry was over. When I told Laura what happened, she reacted like anyone would that was falsely accused: it just built on the dancing issue and all we could do was politely withdraw from doing that vital ministry.

## YOGA, MEDITATION, AND OTHER TERRIBLE THINGS

In 20 years of ministry, I have never had anyone refuse to take communion from me. But this guy quietly told me he was not going to accept what we called *The Lord's Supper*. I said, "okay" suspiciously, to which he replied, "I'll talk to you later about it." Sure enough, we had supper later that week and he told me he didn't like the fact that Laura and I did yoga. It did not matter that he failed to understand what we were doing or anything like that, he was just dead set against it. I explained that he has a right to disagree, but I was not going to change what I'm doing. I told him that judgmental things like this were starting to wear on me and I was considering getting out of the ministry. That would turn out to be a prophecy that came true later.

This wasn't the first thing he questioned me about, and it wouldn't be the last. I don't have a problem with people disagreeing with me. But, when the focus is "either you change or I'm going to make an issue about it," it is no longer a difference of opinion, it is an issue of control. Another leader in the church felt the same way about yoga, and she tried to incite the women against us. Consequently, a couple of these women were also Laura's friends—and then they weren't. It was the beginning of the end in several ways.

No one ever sat down and said, "Help me understand your viewpoint," they were just intent on changing my mind. To be fair, it was mainly their fear that the ministry would somehow be hurt, but they didn't trust my judgment and they didn't trust the Spirit to lead; they had to take control for fear of what might happen.

When you add to these years of inner circles, secret meetings, and various experiences of exclusion, it finally becomes too much. I resigned from the church and again sought solace in a larger church which really didn't heal the wounds, it just gave us a little space to examine them. But eventually we stopped going to church altogether.

There were too many triggers, too many memories, and the armor we had donned was about worn down.

I also wish I could say our experience is abnormal, but it's not. The pain of ministry is real. For many reasons, including that the church is an organization, occasionally there is fallout – both intentional and unintentional. People, including the clergy, get hurt and then they hurt each other.

## *Laura*

I am going to preface this chapter by saying that my emotions are very raw when it comes to the spiritual trauma I endured during our ministry. I am in no way going to apologize for what I am going to write. This is the voice I kept silent for over twenty years. I kept her (my voice) quiet when everyone else could speak hateful and hurtful things. Now, it is her turn, and I am going to honor her and let her speak her truth. I'm going to let her be authentic, brave, and courageous. No apologies.

There must be some sort of invisible human shield that others believe pastors and their families possess. I'm fairly sure everyone thought that our feelings were impenetrable, or that we were made of some sort of superhero caliber like Wonder Woman and could simply deflect any poisonous arrows that came our way. The truth is pastors, and their families are just like any other human being's walking this planet. We have feelings and emotions, and if you send hurtful words or glances our way, they leave very deep, very real wounds.

As I read over what Karl wrote in this chapter, I remember each instance as if it happened yesterday. Some of these incidents happened twenty years ago. So, let me just caution all of us here: the vile and hurtful things we say in the heat of the moment, those things we say to prove our point no matter how hurtful it may be, those things may be said in a split second, but can stay with a person as deep scars for a lifetime. I will not repeat any of what he said, but I will say "yes" to all of it.

I know there is so much talk these days about women in ministry. Pastors, like Beth Moore and Sarah Bessey, have a strong, courageous, and much needed voice in the church today. I am grateful that these women will not allow middle age, white men to silence them from speaking their truth. That said, the most hurtful things I have ever experienced in the church were from women.

Let me back up a little bit. Much of church ministry was very lonely for me. We went from living in big cities such as Dallas and Omaha, to moving to a small town in Southeast Nebraska with a population of 250 people! Talk about culture shock! I had never lived in a small town before Karl started his ministry. When we moved there, I had three young children. J.D. was five, Abbey was two, and Lily was six months old. Being a mom to three young people, in a new small town, where I knew no one, was very lonely. Karl was there, but he was also building up a fledgling church (which is part of his story). He has always been called in to resurrect the struggling churches. So, he was gone a lot. This was also his first church and he wanted to do his best! Much of that was probably our fault for not setting boundaries, but honestly, we didn't know any better. We would learn that lesson soon enough.

So, back to being a young mom with three young babies in a town where I knew no one. The church became my place where I could connect with other women. This was not a problem. Whenever we arrived at a new ministry, it seemed like the women were incredibly happy I was there. Maybe they were just happy to have a "pastor's wife." There were expectations of me that I had no intention of fulfilling. Not because I was stubborn, but because it wasn't who I am. I wasn't going to happily oversee the nursery, I didn't feel led to lead a women's bible study, and I didn't play anything but chopsticks on the piano. Eventually, I did two of the three things—I never played the piano, but I did interact with a lot of women.

As the years passed and Karl began to make some tough decisions that he felt were best for the growth of the church, many began to dig in their heels. The thing about men is they are known for saying what they think, for better or for worse. Some discussions got heated, but Karl has the right temperament to deal with it. Women, however, have a much different way of dealing with things. They whisper. They make sideways comments about your husband. They completely ignore you. Women have a way of finding your most fragile insecurity and pouncing on it. For me, that was being ignored. Much of that wound came from my father, but like I said, some scars, when continually wounded, reopen. Like any scar tissue that is opened, healing takes much longer, and the scars become more vulnerable with each trauma.

Sadly, this was not just at the first church. This happened at every church we pastored. What was worse, the time of each wounding became shorter and shorter at each church we went to. The first church took years for the women to show their true colors; the last church took literally six months! I hope I never understand why this happened or continues to happen because it is not excusable, it is unacceptable. Pastors, their wives, and their families are people with real feelings.

While I have done some personal work to heal from these wounds, I will tell you that I struggle to this day to find total forgiveness for how the women of the church treated, spoke to, and whispered about my husband and especially my children. I heard the things these women said about my husband because they said them to me! They were hoping I would go home and tell Karl how it should be—that somehow, I would take their side over my husband's. I can deal with the hurt from that. What I still struggle with is how this all affected my children. Recently my son said, "I saw how they treated you." Those words still bring a lump in my throat. I never knew they saw those things. I still struggle to forgive the people that caused my children to bear these things.

As a pastor's wife I never quite knew where I fit in, maybe because I was never meant to "fit in." Instead, I now feel like I belong. I belong here, in this moment, to speak my truth and to be there for other pastor's wives and children who have been wounded by spiritual trauma. I want to say to them, and others who have been hurt by people in the church:

You are seen.

You are heard.

You are valuable.

You are enough.

# 8

# HOW RELIGION RUINS SEX

## *Karl*

I don't remember the name of the movie, but I remember that it motivated me to action. I wanted the best for my daughters, and I was confused through most of their time in middle school and high school days. This show was about promise rings and partnering with your child to keep them "pure." It was beautifully motivated, even if it was a little misguided. I devised a plan to give each of my daughters a purity ring and a little speech that I was on their side. When I handed them the ring, their look was stoic, and I never saw the rings again. To this day, none of us have spoken of this event.

One primary problem with the purity culture was that its motivation is fear. I pondered, what would happen if one of my children became pregnant? Girls wonder, what if people begin to think of me as a slut? Most people question, what if I make God mad? Church leadership families worry, what if I displease the church or its members? The church has often used fear as a motivator to keep the parishioners in line. Fear does produce results and helps control the people in the church, but it really doesn't achieve anything noble. People are doing things for all the wrong reasons. We are trying not to do something wrong instead of growing into the person we could be.

Most of the time that I was a pastor, abstinence education was in vogue. This messaging really just amounted to the same thing as the "just say no" drug mantras. We didn't teach young people what it meant to have a healthy relationship or, God forbid, what a healthy sex life looked like. We critiqued the public school system for carrying the ball of sex education, while the church mainly kept silent except for the message of "just keep yourself pure" and "don't do it!"

There was also damaging messaging in the purity culture and evangelical circles. One prominent message was that *boys can't control themselves*. Therefore, all the responsibility rests on the woman to not provoke them with immodest clothing. But the messages went further than that. After Christians are married, women are told that their bodies are not their own and they must submit to their husbands whenever they desire.

With all the confusing messages in Christian culture, it's a wonder to me that we ever had a natural, fulfilling sex life. The shaming messaging and the proliferation of misinformation really never worked at all. It just left us with a culture of sexual misconduct, marital strife, and frustration on all sides.

I wish we could teach boys and girls that the desire they feel for the person they are attracted to is natural. This desire is so strong because it is leading you to something that can be beautiful and fulfilling and complimentary. I want children and adults to understand that the shame they are feeling was heaped on them because someone else was afraid and wanted to control them for their own agenda (such as not being embarrassed).

If I could have a mulligan on the purity rings, I don't think I would have given them to my daughters. The message that prevailed with them was when I told them I loved them and that I believed in them. As best I could, I modeled a relationship with the person I desire, to show them we didn't just have a partnership, we had a relationship. If I could go back, I would tell them that *sex can be one of the most beautiful things you will ever experience. Expect the best, strive for excellence, and for heaven's sake, enjoy the amazing things like sex that are part of being human. Allow yourself to look beautiful and be sexy without feeling guilty or shameful. You are not only spiritual and physical, but also a sexual being! Embrace every part of you that makes you fully human!*

## *Laura*

I definitely want to let Karl off the hook in this chapter. The whole concept of giving a purity ring to our daughters came from me. It's true. I am the one who was filled with shame and fear. Let me rewind a little bit and give you a little bit of my story.

Growing up, sex wasn't discussed in the home. I honestly don't blame my parents. It is just something about which we didn't talk. We learned about our anatomy, and all the changes we would go through as children growing into young men and women, one day at school. That was supposed to be that. We weren't taught about purity or abstinence or even how to have "safe sex." It was simply an anatomy lesson about the changes our bodies were going to go through. However, there was an unspoken sense that sex was "bad" if you did it outside of marriage. Maybe that came from church, although I don't remember hearing anything about "saving yourself for marriage." I honestly do not remember being told this verbatim, but somehow that is the message I received. That really started to solidify when I was in middle school.

I remember being good friends with this girl who was in the eighth grade with me. I can even picture us in class together, sitting by each other, just being kids. While we were both in the eighth grade, she seemed older than me. Her body was more developed. Boys paid a lot of attention to her. I guess I kind of thought it was super cool that boys liked her. I remember she got a boyfriend and she really liked talking to me about him. Our conversations soon turned to sex and how her boyfriend wanted to have sex with her, but she was on the fence about it. I literally had no advice for her! I knew nothing about the topic except that you shouldn't do it until you're married because you could get pregnant.

Well, she did get pregnant. I remember being stunned when she said to me, "I didn't know you could get pregnant the first time you *did it!*" As I have shared in previous chapters, my personality type is a rule follower. When she told me that, I got scared. I thought what she had done was wrong. I remained her friend, but I do remember her just being gone one day. I'm fairly sure she was sent away to have her baby. That memory has stayed with me all these years. It scared me, thinking that all you have to do is have sex one time and you get pregnant. So, my first exposure to sex was strictly anatomical. My second encounter with it was absolute fear. Sounds healthy, right?

Now bring in high school, boys, and dating. For the most part, I had a really good time in high school, although I would not go back if given the chance! There were football games and drill team performances, which were lots of fun! My parents at this time were divorced and my mom had to go back to work. I am in no way blaming anything on my parents! I do hope you hear that! However, the only people I talked to about sex were friends—not the best source.

I remember hearing my friends talk about sex and how it was great, and everyone should do it. I heard that, but there was still that part of me that somehow heard "this is bad and don't do it!" Couple natural feeling and hormones kicking in with an internal voice that tells you this is bad, and you become a hot mess when it comes to sex. Sex becomes secretive. It becomes something you do, but you don't have any clue what you are doing. You are constantly fighting your body to suppress what is simply normal.

So, let's fast forward to those purity rings. That was my fear and shame spewing out all over my daughters. And can I just say right here, right now: why didn't we give our son a purity ring? I'm shaking my head at that one! Sadly, we were perpetuating the purity culture in only presenting them to our daughters. We were implying that it was their responsibility to keep the boys at arm's length and this purity ring, coupled with modest dress, would be some sort of magic shield. Ridiculous! In addition, when we gave them this purity ring, we didn't really explain anything about sex to them. We failed. Was this ring just supposed to magically keep them pure without any explanation?

Here is the bottom-line regarding purity culture: It messes you up! If I could do it all again, I would do it differently. Somehow, my girls seem like they are strong when it comes to their sexuality. I hope that is true. For me, purity culture still affects me. Those whispers still speak to me even though Karl and I have been married for over 30 years. The truth is, we can't tell our children or any young person that sex is "bad" or "wrong" and somehow that mysteriously changes the minute you say, "I do." Sex is not a switch you turn off and then on. We can't be told looking sexy is not ok before marriage and then it's ok after marriage.

Sex is huge! It's not something you just take out at certain times or in certain situations. It is part of who we are. It is vital that we help our children love every part of themselves, and that what they feel at various times is completely normal. It is not a shameful part of them—it is a part of what makes them beautiful.

It's time we do better.

9

# THE ROLE OF WOMEN

## *Karl*

My mother is a strong person. I have heard her talk about having low self-esteem, and while that may have been true, she raised five children without much support. My dad worked hard, but he never developed the skills to lead us effectively. Most of us were raised in systems that stressed the man as the head of family, but often that is only a figurative assumption. Women, like my mother, were the true leaders of the family.

As I began to work in the real world, I often had female supervisors. When I named my first daughter, I named her after several strong women I knew named Abby or Abigail. Several of my doctors, including my current primary care physician, are women. Good and bad, some of the strongest influences on my life have been female.

When I reentered religious life, I opted for a denomination that was the most comfortable for me. Most of these churches are at least autonomous, but they generally opt for pastoral staff leadership, undergirded by a "deacon" board that has some administrative authority. Often, they will have other committees or even a church council that operates with various levels of authorities. But one thing is always a constant: The pastors, and especially the senior pastors, are only male. The deacons and Elders (if they have them) are men. If a woman has a pastoral role (over women and children only), then she may be called a "director" or some other inferior title. Women very rarely speak or preach in my church of origin, even though some immensely popular teachers, like Beth Moore, are from my denomination.

The seminary I attended followed this pattern and the first church I served was governed by a male board. We had an all church meeting several times a year, but most decisions were made by the board. Our second church was a little more congregational. So, although we had a deacon board, it had less influence, and the more regular congregational meeting allowed more input into the day-to-day decisions. Since we were replanting the third church, I was able to organize the church how I wanted, so I rewrote some of the constitution to organize around a board of committee chairpersons. There was a treasurer, the building and grounds chair, the worship leader, plus a couple of elected at large members chosen annually. The fact that it was largely female frustrated the former pastor that attended our church, but it wasn't up for debate.

I know all the debates that we can make concerning what Scripture says and doesn't say. If I wanted to go back 150 years, I could probably have the same discussion about black people's right to vote or be free. One hundred years ago, we would be fighting over women's right to vote. And fifty years ago, we would be demonstrating for or against civil rights for people of color. We can keep having these same debates over and over, or we can just accept that this is one of the last frontiers of the truth that all people are created equal. No one is superior to the other, regardless of sexual orientation, race, country of origin, social status, or gender. We have to stop putting people in boxes so that we feel intimacy because we minimize the same things.

In my opinion, we have missed so much by minimizing what women can do. I have been blessed by so many sermons, speeches, and books over the years, but I wonder how much beauty and wisdom and inspiration I missed because somebody's voice was silenced, because they were born with a vagina. I often tell Laura that she is better than me. There are so many things she does that I can't even begin to do as well as her. She is a better speaker and writer. She is much more disciplined than me. I can't even imagine what she would have accomplished if society and the church wouldn't have subtly told her to be quiet and that her opinion didn't matter as much as the men of the church and our society.

Laura always talks about the fact that much of her pain was caused by women in the church. I always wonder why that was. Maybe it was because they were hurt and hurt people hurt other people. If we believe the generalizations, maybe women are just naturally caddy and manipulative, and they just can't help themselves but to hurt each other. Or maybe, it's because they have been marginalized and minimized by the church and society. Maybe, their voice never really was heard, and they were just trying to speak up for themselves in a way.

I'm not going to argue anymore about whether women should be able to preach, lead, speak, and have positions of power. I'm just assuming, not only that they should, but that they must in times like these. I think I will spend the second half of my life doing what I can to enable this to happen. We need their voice and their leadership now more than ever.

## *Laura*

Like Karl, I come from great stock when it comes to women in my family. I'm going to start with my maternal grandmother. Her name was Lilian. I have so many great memories of her unconditional love. I remember spending Sundays with her as our family went there for lunch every week after church. I remember vividly her being in a dress (probably the one she wore to church), with her apron on, baking her mouthwatering baked beans and biscuits (my mouth is literally watering as I write this. They were that good! I remember she loved tea and I would sit at the table with her and my mom while they drank tea and talked. These memories bring a smile to my face even now. I loved her deeply; so much so that we named our youngest daughter after her. She was strong and beautiful and was truly non-judgmental toward her grandchildren.

That brings me to my mom. I have always admired my mom. She has always been hard working and doing whatever she can for her children, grandchildren, and now great-grandchildren. I don't know the whole story, but she and my dad had a hard marriage. I remember when they were separated and then divorced, my mom worked tirelessly to be sure we girls had everything we needed and much of what we wanted.

My older sister and I were on the drill team. For those of you who don't know what that is, it is important in Texas! It is a team of girls who kick high and do in-air splits during halftime performances of a football game. My younger sister was a cheerleader. Again, a big deal in Texas! All these activities cost lots of money, and for a single mom to be able to give that to us is huge! She worked many hours and worked her way up in the corporate world to be sure we had these things and more. I remember as a teenager writing a paper about the person I most admired and I wrote about my mom. She was selfless and courageous, and she still is.

I'm going to keep going so you really see the big picture of the hearty stock of women I come from. I have two sisters. My older sister lost her husband when they were both 48 years old. I'll never forget the phone call because it rocked my world. Gary was an officer in the Air Force. He had just been given a clean bill of health. He loved boxing and did it frequently. He worked out often. One day, while working out, he died suddenly of a heart attack. I have seen my sister rise from that. I have learned so much from her about living with grief. I have learned so much from her about deep love. She has since remarried an amazing man who understands and supports her need to still remember and love Gary, and to speak of him and share about him as often as she needs. Lisa is strength personified.

I also have a younger sister who has been through a lot—I mean a lot! I have seen her repeatedly pick herself up and find her truth. I have seen her completely be lost as to who she was, only to see her today not willing to compromise her true authentic self for anyone. She has taught me so much about courage, authenticity, and rising strong from the lies we believe about ourselves. Karen exudes grace, both for others and herself.

Finally, I have two amazingly strong, independent, courageous daughters. Most days I look at them in amazement because I am sure they did not get all of that from me.

So, that's my legacy with strong women. They have always been around me. However, in the church, I saw two different roles when it came to women in leadership. The first role was that women had a place, but it was always behind the scenes. In our various church ministries, most women helped in the nursery, cooked in the kitchen, and helped with the worship team. In fact, those were the areas I "ministered" to as well. I also led a bible study—a women's bible study. However, I don't want to give you the idea that the women of these churches were meek and soft spoken.

As Karl alluded to, most of my pain inside the church came from women—women who wanted to be in charge. When they couldn't get their way, they often did whatever they needed to do to achieve their goals. I agree with Karl that hurt people do hurt people, but I also got the strong feeling that in order to get Karl to see things and do things their way, they would go through me. The thing is, I fully supported the vision Karl had. This did not sit well with these strong women, and thus very hurtful actions ensued. I would be completely ignored or not invited to various activities. It was like one day I was "in" and the next day I was "out."

As I shared earlier in this book, I struggled with loneliness during our ministry. I was raising three small children and the church was my only community in these small towns. When that was taken from me, a very lonely experience became even more isolating. These women made accusations about my husband and were not quiet about letting me know how they felt. Some professed to be my "best friend," only to completely disown me when things weren't going their way. Some of the offenders were the pastor's wives, which I still don't understand.

To this day I have never received an apology or any type of closure for these behaviors. I have learned to come to grips with that, although as I write this chapter, it is still painful. I am going to have generous assumptions about these women. I am going to believe that they were and are still hurt and cannot find the words to apologize. I am going to assume that they are caught up in an organization that won't allow them to grow beyond where they were. Having these generous assumptions does not in any way mean I condone their behavior. In fact, I have pity for them, and I do hope that one day they can come to grips with how they have treated others in what they perhaps thought was doing "God's work."

I can't help but wonder how it might have been different if all people were treated equally within the church. Maybe, if women didn't experience this discrimination, they would not feel as much like they had to subvert the system. Possibly, if we could stop hurting women and demoting them, they would rise to greater heights and help us heal our wounded past.

I have had to move on, but I do so with strength: strength to love from a distance, strength to forgive the painful actions but learn from them, and strength to put up boundaries that I am not willing to compromise. Pain has made me a quite different person than who I want to be. I am kind of sad about that, especially because I still believe that church could be different.

I can't wait to see what happens in the near future!

# 10

# THE NEED FOR CONTROL

## *Karl*

Fear and control are two things I never considered while studying to be a pastor. There were never any blatant charges to keep the congregation under control, although most of my examples demonstrated some element of this. In contrast, I was taught about the Holy Spirit that was supposed to be in control, and I could just be "filled with the Spirit" and let the Spirit work. I learned that from Charles Stanley, and it appealed to me. I saw in Scripture where it seemed to always be saying things like "don't be afraid" and "fear not" and "let not your heart be troubled!" Regardless of any intentions that I had, as a pastor, I dealt with fear and control almost every week.

It always happened right before the sermon. Someone would give me something to be "concerned" about. That's why they brought it to my attention, so I could share their concern (fear) and, hopefully, do something about it (control). Church meetings were mostly just a concentrated worry session where we were trying to gain back control of as much as we could. To be fair, any organizational meeting is mostly about these things. That's why, since the American church is an organization, it is almost impossible not to be deeply acquainted with fear and control when doing her business.

I would love to deny it. You may even think I'm bashing the church by saying it. But just because it is disguised as mission statements and objectives, doesn't mean it is not rooted in fear and control. If you don't believe me, just consider the following things. I don't mind being wrong. In fact, I hope that I am. But from its inception, organized religion has created systems that increase our capacity to control, so that we fear less.

## THE MESSAGE

I love good storytelling and a good sermon, I really do! Over the course of my life, when I wasn't preaching, I had the privilege to listen to some genuinely great preachers. I went from being a person that couldn't lead a silent prayer to someone that loved communicating through the spoken word. I still love it, I still miss it, but there are some things I didn't realize until I stepped away.

Back when I was failing speech in college, I learned about persuasive speech. Later, I learned about it again in Toastmasters when I was honing my skills. I can't remember the structure I learned, but I know what I did almost instinctively by listening to other speakers, and especially pastors. First, there is a time of putting people at ease and letting them know they can trust you—that you're on their side. That could be called the *ethos.* The second part is the *pathos.* It is where the speaker presents you with a problem you may or may not have known you had. It's effective when you didn't even know you had the problem because the speaker appears to be that much more intuitive. This is deliberately followed by the presentation of the solution in Scripture and modern and ancient literature or other illustrations. The last part is the appeal to logic, or *logos*. In other words, it would be negligent to not agree with the speaker's proposition, amen?

I never intended to play on people's fears, but that is often what I was doing in a sermon. It is what leaders do in an organization even if they don't know they are doing it. Even if it's just that people feel like they are in danger of losing connection to people, leaders tend to assure them that "we're your family" or "you're on the right team" or "that's why you come here." Sometimes people need this for reassurance, but within an organization, it's too easy to resort to shaming and inadvertently manipulate people in a large group.

Another question that is being discussed lately is the idea of only one person speaking at the main service on Sunday. Why is this so? Why do we do this? It's just what we've always done. Even in churches where there are more than one teaching pastor, only the designated people speak. Many in home churches are challenging this myth and allowing people to speak as they are led to speak. How can we possibly receive a rich, vibrant view of how the Spirit is working if we only hear from one person? On the other hand, if we let just anyone speak, then who knows what would happen? So, because we are afraid, we control the situation and Pastor Karl always did all the speaking. We probably missed a lot.

## THE MEMBERSHIP

I was a pastor in small churches. The general pattern for me was to take a struggling, new, or replanted church, and build them up to about 70 to 100 people. That's small by megachurch standards. But one of my consistent fears was, "What if no one shows up?" or "what if they all leave?" Usually, the absence of a few families could wreck the whole thing. We needed somewhat of a consistent membership to attend regularly to make the organization function. Part of my focus always had to be on getting them there and making sure they stayed there. There's a lot of fear and control in that part of the story.

But not only did I have to be "concerned" with attendance, but also with their behavior once they got there. One person tended to take over things. Another liked to shoot holes in everything. Some people were just rude and condescending. The fear of everything "getting out of hand" was a common discussion. If that happens, what is next? Early on in my pastoral career, someone convinced me I had to "do something" about someone, so I marched over there and screwed it up even worse. My attempts to control people almost never had the desired effect.

The real problem with controlling behavior is that, in an organization, shame is the primary tool to modify behavior, and it can be extremely damaging to church members. People have lasting wounds from being shamed at church. So, mix fear with a deficient system of handling crisis, and you have a church that consistently produces wounded individuals that either wound each other or move on to another place without healing. People wounded in community must find healing in community, but it's very seldom that it happens in churches because the systems there make it hard to be vulnerable. If possible, the organization will bypass the issue and do its best to get back to work and not think about it too much.

It takes a certain amount of people to make an organization run. So, while someone walks out one door, we are shaking hands with the one coming in the other door. We do a little to keep them happy, but mostly we hope they'll just pay the tithe, do something to help without causing problems or asking too many questions, and all will be well. Our fears mixed with our outdated models make it very unlikely we won't just keep shuffling through people to keep the organization running. To totally re-engineer the enterprise, we have committed to, would be way too frightening. So, we soldier on and call it faithfulness when it's often just a fear of the unknown and a reluctance to do much of anything vastly different than we have always done.

## THE MEETING

One day, at my first church, I pulled up all the chairs and stacked them against the back wall of the church. When people came in, I invited them to come up front and just worship without the chairs. Another time I switched the order of service where I preached first, then we sang. It wasn't really all that radical, but it frightened people. I don't think they could even articulate what they were afraid of, but to alleviate this, we went back to the normal order of service. Most times when I deterred from the order, people subtly nagged me back into returning to the way it used to be. We like things to be as we expect, or it often worries us.

As I discussed before, the traditional and contemporary once-a-week services in most churches is a show. I don't apologize for that statement—it's not derogatory. It just is what it is. The "show" is designed to elicit a particular response; it is rehearsed, it is structured, and even though it may not be anything like Jesus imagined, it limits people's fear response and produces a feeling similar to comfort food, because we know what to expect. We come back week after week to get our fix and feed the machine.

After service, I always stood at the back and shook people's hands. The most common response was, "good message." That was my fix. I needed a certain amount of appreciation. I needed people to be there each week to alleviate my fears of not being needed or effective or whatever I was thinking at the time. They also thanked me for other various things, but mainly they said to me in various ways, "That was what I was expecting, but it was in a way that made me happy." They never thanked me for moving the chairs, but they often thanked me for hitting the target that suited them.

## THE MONEY

I made it a point to almost never speak about money in my sermons, but we did talk about it at every board meeting because we were afraid of a lot of things. Most of the reasons are obvious, so I won't go into them all.

I heard about a good church for young people when my daughter moved to a certain town. I drove up and took her and her husband to this hip and growing congregation. The teaching pastor of the day was young and well spoken, and he used all those things to preach incessantly about giving to the church. My daughter said she felt like they only wanted her money. They haven't been back to church since. She was already a little anti-church but that definitely didn't help.

As an organization, to say that we are not concerned (afraid) that the money will stop coming in would be lying. Whatever tactic the organization takes, it is dealing with fear and trying to control the flow of money into the church. With bigger budgets, buildings and bathrooms, the fears and need for control only get more complex. I would never deny that money matters, but it still just amplifies the tendency to fear and the implied need to control. The better we "handle" it, the more addicted to it we become.

I'm not saying there is not a need for reasonable awareness and responsibility. But, when we make the church an organization, it just becomes inevitable that fear and control become two of the most dominant issues in the church that rob the assembly of its vibrancy and mystery and beauty. I think we can do better.

## *Laura*

I'll be honest with you; I never gave much thought to the ins and outs of church life. Karl was always good at keeping track of the message, the membership, the meeting, and the money. On occasion he would have me count how many people were in attendance, but other than that, I didn't take any interest in the organizational aspects of the church. I had seen on occasion the controlling aspects of each of these areas and frankly all it did was create personal anxiety for me. I was busy trying to raise three active children, so all those "M" words were more of Karl's responsibility. My own personal "M" word, I suppose, would be Motherhood.

### MOTHERHOOD

Raising children has been one of the most beautiful things I have had the privilege of doing. I remember the first night we had our son, Jordan, home from the hospital. There was a flood of emotions, but I remember standing over his crib sobbing, saying "He's an angel!" I couldn't imagine this little being had anything, but goodness weaved inside of his tiny body. He taught me everything there was to know about being a mom. There was nursing, which, by the way, no one told me would hurt like hell the first time they latched on. Then, later, the first steps inevitably ended with a goose egg on his forehead and a myriad of scraped knees and bruised elbows. He also taught me that my capacity to love another was infinite. I had no idea.

As our family began to grow, and we added Abbey and Lily, I began to learn some incredible life lessons. I always thought I would teach them, but the surprise was what they taught me. First, it is important to know when to get involved. Sometimes the first inclination is not always the best recourse. Continually rescuing children or solving their problems doesn't always work out the best overall.

Another important lesson was to know when it gets quiet, they are up to something! At one house we lived in, we converted the attic to Abbey's room. One day, she and Lily were secretly using a mattress to slide down the stairs from her room to Lily's room. During the process, Abbey must have miscalculated and banged her head on the nearby wall. I never saw the blood or even the cut!! To this day, she still has the scar to prove that they enjoyed stair sledding when they were younger.

The last lesson I learned from them is it is important to choose your battles, especially as they grow older. Jordan had long hair and wore shorts in high school during all four seasons while living in Missouri. I'm talking snow, sleet, and freezing rain, he was in shorts and Vans, with no socks. If I had to guess, he was expressing his independence, and it certainly wasn't hurting anyone. People often remind us, "It's just hair, it's just clothes, it will grow back, that will heal up nicely, most things aren't permanent!" Dressing a little differently probably helped him stand out a little, which isn't all that bad. Now, when I am at school and see a high school student wearing shorts in the dead of winter, it makes me smile just a little bit.

I have so many funny, warm memories of raising my three children, but raising children brings its own set of anxiety producing issues—issues that come with having a dad who is a pastor, and with having a mom who tends to be fearful. Our children were the "Pastor's kids" after all; the church was looking at them and critiquing them. I was sure that their actions would be a direct reflection on me. Small town living didn't help. When you live in a town of 250 people, on a good day, your children are probably going to be watched. Couple that with being a pastor's kid and they will probably be watched with a higher level of scrutiny.

This most assuredly, sent me into protection mode. It was part of my job as a mom to protect our family's reputation from the judgment of others. It was my duty to be sure our children were at church, dressed and presentable, every time the doors were open. They needed to be in Sunday school, in every production of every biblical play known to man, and as they grew up, they needed to be a part of our church's youth group. In other words, they needed to "look the part." Looking back on that last statement makes me sad. I am contemplating, if I ever once asked them what was going on in their own hearts about this "faith" that I was forcing on them?

I can answer that—No! I was too busy "playing the part" and whether they liked it or not, they were actors in a production they didn't even audition for. I remember vividly both of our girls telling us they didn't like going to youth groups. While we didn't always make them go, sometimes we did because, "the show must go on!"

I am not sure how it happened, but despite my "fear based" parenting, our children learned to think critically. They credit us, but honestly, I do not remember teaching them this skill because I am not sure I was thinking critically during those child rearing years! Maybe Karl did? I don't know. What I do know is I was in protection and preservation mode. However they gleaned this critical thinking, I am glad they did.

Today, they are three amazing adults who can think for themselves. They love exponentially. They speak up for those oppressed and marginalized. They are making beautiful lives for themselves in their areas of the world and beyond. Not one of them attends church right now and I'm ok with that. I think, much like my earlier parenting, church can stifle creativity and critical thinking. We are told what to think and when to think it. Our children have never been willing to sit inside that box. Nope. They would rather push the boundaries and wear shorts in the dead of winter. They would rather ride a mattress down the attic stairs. They would rather experience things fully and firsthand. There is so much freedom in that.

Do I still get scared for them sometimes? Do I still call them to see if they made it home from work or a doctor's appointment safely? Most definitely! I'll never stop being concerned for them, but today it is a healthy concern rather than a fear based, "What will people think?" mentality.

As I look back on motherhood, I can't help but wonder if my best moments weren't what I started when I looked upon their preciousness as I saw them for the first time. All my efforts to control them probably didn't help them nearly as much as the simple fact that I adore them and love them with all my heart. In the book of Genesis, God said, "It is very good" when He looked at His children. Maybe we would be a lot better off in our churches and schools and families if we simply looked at each other with love, compassion, and gratefulness instead of wondering how to control them so we won't be afraid as much.

PART 2

# *Finding Our Way in the Desert*

## 11

# FINDING COMMUNITY IN THE DESERT

### *Karl*

When I try to discuss the topics in this book, the most prominent pushback that I get from those that attend church is in the area of community. They will say to me, "But, we need community!" And I will say, "I couldn't agree more." But, if we all agree that community is important, maybe it would be worth our time to go through an assessment and make sure we are all talking about the same thing and have a good understanding of what a good community looks like.

There are moments I remember quite vividly in the over two decades of church work. There was the time, early in my ministry, where I reached out to a family in need and found myself performing the ceremony for a 16-year-old boy that was killed in a car wreck. We got even closer that year when his cousin also died in a car wreck. I was instantly a part of their community, not by choice, but because of our circumstances. When you step back and analyze those experiences, you only make one assessment, "That was extremely difficult, but it was also extremely rich and good and beautiful."

In 20 years, I suppose I attended at least twenty graduations. I probably officiated 20 to 30 weddings, and at least that many funerals. Especially in my first church, I was there for everything: the fish fry's, the community Christmas parties, and the street dance that got me in trouble. At the second church, we cooked breakfast for the campers nearby and experienced a different kind of transient community, but it was community, nonetheless. Our last church was in Nebraska City, Nebraska where the important thing was the Applejack Festival. So, being a part of that community meant being in parades with the Christian motorcycle group, and going to their meetings, and trying to help meth addicts and homeless people get back on their feet. But more than anything, in all the churches, community meant responding to the needs of the people that came across the threshold of the church. It's easier in the smaller church, but I don't suppose the mission changes no matter how big the church is.

### WHY DO WE NEED COMMUNITY?

Community helps us *advocate* for each other. As communities grow that have similar interests, and they gain confidence to speak up for each other. We want someone to "have our back" when we don't have the energy or resources to fight for ourselves. Groups help gently educate each other about their personal challenges, so often members with similar interests often develop compassion for each other's unique challenges.

This is what gave me the greatest joy as a pastor. Much like a family, when people were a part of our community church, we felt a special need to get involved when we normally wouldn't. Some of the people we advocated for admitted they were about to give up hope that they could overcome their situation. But, with community, everyone gains confidence to overcome challenges. It is a good kind of groupthink, I suppose.

Not only do we speak up for those in our community, but we *support* and *protect* them. Because the group gives us a sense of belonging, it becomes almost a requirement that we would give time and resources to the group and, if necessary, risk something of ours to protect them. The longer the relationship lasts, the stronger these bonds become. Even introverts appreciate a support system.

This is especially helpful in times of struggle. I can't tell you how many times we have cried with and counseled people in distress. Maybe, one of the toughest parts of going through a deconstruction is that my support system has been fragmented. Although I'm building a new community, it is a little less structured and maybe a little more fragile.

Hopefully, another advantage of community is that we grow in *wisdom*. As the group faces challenges, hopefully it learns from its successes and failures. It is beautiful to see a church or other organization that becomes better and better over time. I love to learn by myself, but hopefully wisdom is multiplied when we grow together. I think one reason for this is that we all see things differently. Community helps us see and hear and observe from multiple vantage points so that growth is optimal.

A few days ago, we did a podcast with several of our newest friends. We were talking about the issues in this very book. I was amazed and humbled by how these people from all occupations, and multiple situations, could bring such depth to the conversation, while all showing the different vantage points their lives offered.

One of the participants was talking about church and exclaimed, "This is my church—you people are my church!" What he meant is that this online community has become *his* community. It was supplying a necessary infusion of the support he needed while giving him a place to contribute. It's a community, simple, unadulterated by the organization.

### DANGERS IN COMMUNITY

The most obvious danger in the community is *abuse*. This happens when people take advantage of the loyalty and trust that a group offers. Communities thrive on a certain amount of trust. We open up and give people our trust so that they can help and support us. It's absolutely necessary to take risks in order to love. Love makes us vulnerable. Being brave puts us at risk of getting hurt no matter what the context. When people take advantage of our vulnerability, they are abusing the trust we have given them. It is not that religious systems promote abuse, but they sometimes give abusers a cloak under which to operate. Families often have the same vulnerable relationships that can hide similar instances of abuse.

As a pastor, I have dealt with the fallout of abuse. In my humble opinion, the biggest issue with resolving these types of issues is *spiritual bypassing*. We want easy answers and catch phrases and simple resolutions. But rebuilding trust takes time and energy and understanding. It's an incremental journey, not a miraculous transformation. I am sure God can change our attitude in an instant, but years of pain and neglect and abuse takes even longer to rebuild. People must be seen with eyes of grace and find graceful, loving people that restore them slowly.

Between our second and third church, we took a couple of years off before planting another church. We found the best place to *hide out,* religiously, was in the third row of the church. We filed into church at the right time and left at the right time, and if we wanted to, avoided all human contact. Anything personal we did was when we chose to do it; there were no inconveniences, no impositions, no painful struggle with other people—no community! When I lived in a small town, I couldn't avoid the town folk; they knew everything about me, including when I got the mail. Communities can be places where my gifts and talents are expressed, or they can be places where I blend into the point of anonymity.

One of the unfortunate draws of the community is what Brene' Brown calls "Common Enemy Intimacy." She explains:

> "Common Enemy Intimacy is counterfeit connection and the opposite of true belonging. If the bond we share with others is simply that we hate the same people, the intimacy we experience is often intense, immediately gratifying, and an effortless way to discharge outrage and pain. It is not, however, fuel for real connection."[14]

Community becomes quite simple when we get together to talk about who we don't like. American politics facilitates this "us versus them" mentality. But, as Brown stresses, "hating the same people" is really a "counterfeit connection" and not really what we truly need from communities. It may make us feel good, but it's not a real community. It's easier to talk about what we are against, but it's much more noble to talk about what we are for. Real community is when we do the challenging work of understanding and celebrating our differences. Churches tend to cluster like-minded people and focus on differences with the *other* people.

There is another subtle danger in the community that might be loosely connected with the "main thing." Often corporate goals in a community like church (we call them mission statements), can cause the organization to not acknowledge people's individual challenges.

---

**14** Brown, Brene, *Braving the Wilderness: The Quest for True Belonging and the Courage to Stand Alone.* New York: Random House, 2017, 136

Sometimes communities and churches don't have time for us to express our pain and not be "okay." Spiritual bypassing tempts us to find easy solutions for people's pain, and catchphrases to pacify the hurting. In a true community, it has to be okay for people not to be okay for a season. When I lead a contemplative group, I have to keep reminding them not to fix people's problems, and just let them be where they are.

Even if our community is a great community, there needs to be a chance for people to take some time off. If it's not okay to leave, then we need to ask the question "why?" Are we afraid that we can't control people after they get outside the immediate influence of the group? That sounds more like a cult than a community. The things we really love, we set free (metaphorically or actually) and let them see us from the outside. True community is not controlling and should allow us some room to breathe occasionally. I knew minimally about the communities when I was a part of them, but the only way I really knew them was to get away from them. When I missed them, then that was truly my community. When I felt better being outside of them, it was probably a good indication to keep going.

## WHERE WE FIND COMMUNITY

Several months ago, when we stopped going to church, the most common injunction from people was, "Community is important." As I said before, "I couldn't agree more." The best way I can answer this issue is to describe my current communities. That's right, it's plural. I don't think any of us just have one community.

At the moment, every day I drive to work at a large hardware store. I do a very physical job where we make sure the professional contractors get what they need. I drive forklifts and physically load products and make sure the person has another person to talk to. It's a little like a church. I greet them coming in and help them, then I send them on their way with "have a wonderful day." My partner, Kenny, and I do the grumpy old man routine and usually bring a smile to people's faces when we poke fun at each other—like the old guys in the Muppet Show. It's not what I want to do forever, but right now it's part of my community.

Another part of my community is a group of podcasters and authors. My publisher is Quoir, and I couldn't be happier to be associated with them. We all try to help promote each other's books and it's just a place where we all are in about the same boat and understand each other's struggles. The other podcasters and bloggers that I meet online have some similar interests and discuss things with which we are struggling.

I would encourage someone who doesn't think that the online experience can provide community, to host a podcast and interview someone for 45 minutes. Or just interview someone and discover how fruitful it is for the soul. It is impossible not to be closer to someone after you truly listen to them for that length of time. I hear Laura saying, "Amen!" in the background. My friend, Jason Elam, says, "This is my church—these are my people!"

Another part of my community is the HeartConnexion community. Laura and I have participated in the BreakThrough seminars at critical points in our lives. Dr. Paul and Susanna Fitzgerald have been consistent beacons in our lives to guide us back to the true North. It's not uncommon to reach out to them as I navigate the path that I'm on. Several members of this community provide support and encouragement at various points in our life. They are part of our community.

The most interesting part of my community is my family. Our three children and their families are one of the most comforting parts of my life. When they are here visiting, I experience a peace that must be from God or if it isn't, don't tell me different. My siblings and my mother are eternal to me. I will always love them, but we live different lives in various places. If they arrived at my door, I would do whatever they needed me to do at any time of the day. If I found out they had committed an egregious crime, I would still love them and support them because they are a part of me. The wonderful thing about a good family is that you don't have to reprove that love at certain intervals. It's just true! They are part of my community in one of the most special ways.

Some people say their spouse is their best friend—I don't say that! I would just say that Laura is primary. For over 30 years, there has been nothing that mattered more than her! So, take that for what it's worth. You could feel compassion for her, because she accepted me in my broken state and she endured all of the transitions, for better or for worse. My image of God is evolving but my image of Laura is growing! Every year that passes, I appreciate her more! Whatever I say about her only diminishes what I feel about her; so, may I just say that she is the primary member of my community. She is not the boss, and she is not the underling, but make no mistake about it, she is first!

## HOW TO JOIN A COMMUNITY

As a final word about community, let me just give a couple of suggestions that were given to me by a moderator of an online community. He suggested that I ask more questions instead of giving advice. In general, he suggested that I should give more than I take. I think that's great advice for joining a community. I often focus on the perfect post, instead of contributing to a post that is already there. The world doesn't always need a new community, but we can make any community better by giving our best to that community.

## *Laura*

The definition of community is, "A group of people living in the same place or having a particular characteristic in common. A feeling of fellowship with others, as a result of sharing common attitudes, interests, and goals."

I'm simply curious why the biggest argument I get from people about not attending an organized worship service (church) is this idea of community. If I am looking at the above definition, from the dictionary, I interpret that to mean that I can find community anywhere! I have a community at my work. I have community within my family. In addition, I have community by myself, if I genuinely believe the Divine is within me.

12

# FINDING MY VOICE IN THE DESERT

## *Laura*

Early in my teaching career, it was not unusual for me to lose my voice at least twice a year. Talking a lot will do that to you. Now that I use a teaching method called Whole Brain Teaching (WBT), I don't lose my voice as often because the idea behind WBT is to do little talking and allow students to be the teachers and teach each other! While I have found a way to save my voice within the teaching profession, I had not realized how stifled my voice had become in ministry.

Perhaps losing my voice started young. I am the middle child and have always had a propensity to be a mediator. I did more listening than debating. I never really felt like I was strong as a child, either. I was somewhat of a sickly child. However, when we entered ministry, and as things became more stressful at our various churches, I found myself sinking into a dark space where my voice was nonexistent.

I vividly remember when Karl finally told me he felt the call into ministry. I say "finally" because when he told me, he said he had been feeling this call for about five years! That's a long time to keep something like that inside. Honestly, when he told me, I didn't have much of a reaction. I thought, "Ok, cool!" Yeah, I know, not exactly a spiritual response. I honestly didn't think a whole lot about it, but I did know that I wanted to support him; especially if God Himself had called him to this. How could I trump God? Who was I to say "no" to God? So, Karl began the process of becoming a great American Evangelical pastor. I was a stay-at-home mom to our son, Jordan, but by the time Karl was done with school, we added Abbey and Lily to our family. Although he was working full time and going to school at night for the ministry, I loved our life!

Karl's first pastorate was in a small town of only 250 people. Let me take a step back. I grew up in Rochester, New York—not a small town. My family moved to the Dallas, Texas area when I was 13. It was definitely not a small town! After we were married, we moved to Omaha, Nebraska. Again, not a small town. So, when we moved to Stella, Nebraska for Karl's first church assignment, suffice it to say, it was a huge culture shock. I'm not knocking small towns. Actually, since we moved to Stella, every place we have lived since then has been a small town. Small towns are so quaint. People are friendly and welcoming. People smile and wave. It really is a wonderful, safe place to raise a family. However, if you are the pastor and his/her family in a small town, you live in a fishbowl, and every move you make can be scrutinized under a microscope. For someone who learned early to blend into the woodwork or just stay quiet, this would lead my soul into the perfect storm.

As I said, things started out well at all of our churches. Almost too well. We made friends fast. Almost too fast. I'm not sure it was based on anything I would constitute as a solid friendship. It was basically based on the fact that each of these churches were desperate. They were all failing. They were all on the verge of closing their doors. They were all running twenty members or less on any given Sunday. I have no better way to describe what I feel other than these churches looked at Karl as their savior. He was there to resurrect the dead. Regardless, our family felt welcomed, loved, and accepted at the beginning of each new adventure.

In my mind, as we went into ministry, my thought was, "This is Karl's thing. This is his calling, not mine. I'm not going to be the 'typical' pastor's wife. I don't play the piano or organ, I'm not going to be leading any bible studies, and I am a stay-at-home mom. I'm not doing the nursery!" It was his gig, not mine. So, when things came up that kept him out late at church or called him away from our family, it wasn't my place to say how I felt. Again, who was I to go up against what God had called Karl into? So, I kept my task-at-hand to be raising my babies and I subdued my voice.

When you are in ministry, there are highs and lows. That is true for any career path a person chooses. When the lows came, they hit hard. At our first church, we were encouraged to go to a street dance. This was a yearly dance where the whole community came out to have fun and connect. We were told by various members of our church that it would be great if we could attend. It would give people a chance to get to know who we were, as well as help us get to know people in our community. Everything was going so well, and we were enjoying the night. We always enjoyed slow dancing or two stepping to a great song.

So, when one came on during the street dance, we decided to dance together. I remember looking into each other's eyes and smiling throughout the entire dance. We were both feeling really good about where we were in life and where we were in our community. However, this was short lived. Within the week, the very people that encouraged us to attend the street dance felt it was wrong that we danced while there. This was hard for me to process. I was dancing with my husband, not some stranger. It was a slow dance, our hands were appropriately placed on one another's bodies, and there was zero inappropriate gyrating. I had no idea what we had done wrong, but remember, I said Karl was pastoring a conservative church. Apparently, dancing was still a mistake. We just didn't know the rules. No one told us. We didn't realize we had done anything wrong.

This wasn't the only time we would butt up against legalism. This was only the beginning. With it came incredible shame for me. I was completely embarrassed and felt I had done something so inappropriate by dancing with my husband. I know this sounds extreme, but I honestly felt so exposed by the level of judgment of us that it felt we had done something so much more sinister than simply dancing. It was as if the whole town had caught us having sex in the back seat of our car. This shame shut me down and silenced my already silent voice even further.

There were issues at both our other churches, as well. Both began the same as Stella. We were there to bring life to a dying church. It was mainly Karl, but now that our children were getting older, I felt like I should be a little more present in these ministry opportunities. I began to lead women's bible studies, sing in the worship band, and helped with various Sunday school and vacation bible school classes. I put myself out there increasingly, which left me very visible and very vulnerable. This was not a comfortable place for me, since I was someone who felt more comfortable blending into the background and just keeping quiet.

At our last two churches, things started to go south so much quicker than they did in Stella, but unlike Stella, the people creating the most trouble were women. They were incredibly vocal, deafening even! Karl was in the process of truly finding his voice and his purpose in ministry. He also had an amazing vision for the church, both local and as a whole. When the women of these churches didn't like what Karl was saying, it became evident they no longer wanted us around. It was so hard to see my husband attacked and misrepresented by these women. However, once again, I felt small. It wasn't my place to say anything. Not to these women, but also, not to Karl. I wanted out of the ministry. Each one was toxic, and each was more toxic than the last. So, I did what I did best. Stayed silent and slid into the background even more.

When we left the ministry, my heart was pretty numb. We had put our whole selves out there at every church. We were left exposed and vulnerable, and even though all we knew going into each ministry was to love with our whole hearts, when we left, I was deeply wounded. However, I never spoke of it. We started going to a pretty big church about an hour from our home. I will admit, at first it was healing. It was a big church; I could get lost in the crowd; I could get lost in the music. As we continued to visit, however, all the feelings and words I had wanted to say for over 20 years were starting to come out, and not very well.

I was questioning the church as a whole. I didn't understand how something that was supposed to welcome the broken and the hurting had created so much brokenness and hurt within me. I could no longer see God and when I did, He was kind of an asshole. I thought we had been through so much crap in the past 20 years at places He was supposed to be, and He just didn't show up for us. We laid it all out for Him. I followed Karl's call. I served beside him faithfully. He served God faithfully. All for what? For a heart that just couldn't take it anymore. I just wanted to be done with church. It was a place of toxicity for me, not a place of healing.

Today, I am still healing. What has helped me most in my healing was the birth of my granddaughter, Hollyn. I was deep in my woundedness when she was born. I vividly remember the ride to the hospital. I could not wait to meet her! When we arrived, it was seconds before she was in my arms. At that moment, everything melted away. It seemed like no one else was in the room with us. Her ear was pressed against my breast. For the first time in forever, I had a heartbeat. She had split my heart wide open in that very instant. What happened next was nothing I would have ever expected. I liken it to a mini, spiritual breakdown.

I remember crying for no reason for about 2 weeks straight at various times. I would just sob and say, "I can't do this!" I would shake and almost hyperventilate. I was a wreck. Little did I know that Hollyn's birth would begin to resurrect my voice. It wasn't a smooth transition. Many things came out sideways. I couldn't articulate my feelings after they had been buried for so long. When I held Hollyn that very first time, it was as if the Divine reached down and said, "This, my child, is how I love you. It is how I have always loved you. You are more than your shame. You are precious. Every part of you. Let me hold you as you heal." Hollyn was absolutely the catalyst to my healing.

On February 14, 2018, we learned that our youngest daughter was pregnant. I was thrilled! Another grandchild and I could not wait! Karl and I were in the process of working on some personal healing through HeartConnexion Ministries. We were just about to go into our immersive weekend where we were going to do some hard work. About 5 minutes before they shut the doors, I got a phone call. Lily had just gone for their 20-week ultrasound. You know, the one where you learn if you are having a boy or a girl! However, their ultrasound showed that there were some issues with their baby. It was hard to process in 5 minutes. I didn't know what to think or feel. I could not pray.

20 years of ministry came rushing back saying, "You better pray, pray hard, and you better use all the right words! If there isn't 'healing,' it's your fault for not praying enough!" However, I couldn't. I didn't feel God. Yes, my heart opened up with Hollyn, but because I still saw God in a very unhealthy way, I really didn't want to talk to Him. We had been through hell and back in ministry and He was pretty distant a lot of the time. Jackson was born in August 2018, two months premature. As we made our way to the hospital, I had no idea what to expect.

When we got there, the room looked vastly different from the room Hollyn was in after her birth. It was dark with lots of monitors beeping and lights flashing. Then, there was little Jackson, all two pounds of him, with tubes going down his throat and monitors checking his every move. He was "contained" in blankets to mimic the womb since he technically wasn't supposed to be out of his mommy yet. He had a mask over his eyes. I remember Lily telling me I could "hold" him. This would be different than holding Hollyn for the first time. To hold Jackson, I could stick my hands into the isolate. We were told not to stroke his skin, but rather, we were to put our hands on him and apply light pressure. This is called "containment."

I remember reaching in. I remember touching his little body. At that moment, I couldn't hold back my tears. They flowed so freely that I felt my shoulders shaking and I left a visible puddle of my tears on the floor. I remember looking over at Lily and Trevor and saying, "I'm sorry." I really wanted to be so brave for them, but at that moment, I couldn't. At that moment, they comforted me, and for the first time I had permission to cry.

The birth of both my grandchildren has been an awakening for me. They have shown me that the image of God that I had was not correct. They have both opened my heart so that the false idea of God could finally leave. Their births were the beginning of the demolition of everything I once knew about God.

## *Karl*

I was excited when Laura started to *find her voice.* Back in my earlier days, even when I was a little more committed to the man as the primary leader in the home, I still wanted Laura to have equal say and an equal voice. The few times that she gave speeches made me wish she could preach, and I could sit in the audience. She has a more natural speaking voice, and she has always had something vital to say. Since I was a preacher and writer, I assumed I was using my voice and nothing much was hindering it. It's amazing how confused we can be in this area. I certainly was. It wasn't until recently that my friend Mark Karris invited me to go a little deeper and I am glad that I did.

Please understand I am not talking about introverts and extroverts. I will most likely always be an introvert. I love people, I just don't want them around all the time. I have friends that are extroverts and introverts, people that talk a lot and people that talk a little. I know natural born speakers, and people that struggle to speak well, especially in public. Even with writers, there is a great mixture of personalities and temperaments. I think finding our voice is something a little deeper than just what we have proclivity toward. In its simplest form, finding our voice may be that we know who we are and how we are learning how to express it.

One thing is for sure: If we don't get to say what we really need to say, our voice goes down into our shadow, and we suffer the consequences of that. Like many other things, when our voice gets pushed down into our shadow, it comes out wrongly and at inopportune times. When I am not speaking from a place of authenticity, I end up speaking my truth to the wrong people at the wrong times and with the wrong attitude. But, why is finding our voice even necessary?

My friend, Mark Karris says,

> "For many of us, it is not just finding our voice, it is sharing it with others that is so powerful. When there is a cacophony of voices all around us, people listening to us helps us feel *safe and alive.* It *validates* our existence and *soothes* our existential angst, especially if we are prone to thinking about our mortality and sheer evaporation from existence in a relatively brief period of time. Sharing our voice with others helps us feel *less alone*, more *connected*, and also provides tremendous *purpose*. Knowing we are making a difference in the world, knowing that our pain, suffering, and divine gems can help someone else, is hugely *rewarding*."[15]

I thought I started finding my voice in college after I almost failed speech class because I forgot half of my 15-minute final speech. I realized I might have a problem that needed to be addressed. A couple of years later, one of my managers called me into her office and told me I did indeed have a problem. She told me I was smart, but if I didn't figure out how to talk (you know, like, to people), then my job was going to be in jeopardy. There was a group/class in the same building that helped people get better at things like that and I joined it. It was excruciating at times (think extemporaneous speaking for recluses), but it was helpful. Years later, I joined a Toastmasters group where I eventually became a leader and won a couple of awards for speaking. Just a brief time after that, I accepted a call to pastor a

---

**15** From an email message while writing this manuscript, February 2020

church and the circle of shyness was complete. Well, not really, I still shook a little every time I spoke, but I figured that was a good thing.

But did I really find my voice? I always considered myself a challenging speaker. I liked to "step on people's toes" a little but do it in a subtle way. I liked to see them have positive changes in their life from what they heard from my preaching. But, when you are preaching to a congregation and especially the same congregation, you only have so much wiggle room in that process. So, although I was challenging people, to a considerable extent I was mainly telling them what they wanted to hear. I was trying to gain the approval of others and find some satisfaction in it. Sure, I overcame my shyness, but I didn't necessarily find my voice. It might have touched some of Mark's bullet points, but not really in any genuine kind of way.

Why didn't I use my voice more effectively in the first half of my life? Did something cause it? My mom's always afraid I'm going to blame stuff on her, but I don't remember my mom directly doing anything dramatic or extremely traumatic. I do think there are some things that are a little bit significant for a boy that used to hide under the table when people came to visit.

Like most children during my era, it was common for children to make fun of each other. Bullying was barely acknowledged. Calling people names and making fun of them was the norm and not the exception. My childhood was full of all distinct kinds of schools and daycares. When you have thick glasses, and you're short, and you sometimes wear funny clothes, it's just kind of natural that you get picked on. At least it was in the time I grew up. Speaking up, or speaking in front of the class, was just another way to get made fun of.

I don't know about anyone else, but I was a little mischievous when I was a boy. Some of the things I remember especially were in Junior High. While attending a private school, I learned how to steal candy at the store, throw water balloons at cars, and eventually smoked a few cigarettes. I didn't like smoking that much, but I adopted smokeless tobacco and retained that habit for the next 30 years or so. The question was not how bad the things we did were, but how did the adults respond to us? When I was in Junior high, the strategy seemed to be either spanking (hitting) or shaming. I remember distinctly the day my mother realized that spanking no longer worked —I told her, "That didn't hurt."

The question about spanking is not whether it works. Spanking definitely gets results. But does it get the right results? What are we teaching kids about the world when we spank them? Just because spanking gets results doesn't mean it accomplishes anything noble. I know this because eventually it stopped working for me. It either creates underlings that eventually aren't afraid of you anymore (like I was), or it finally breaks that person, and they will never be the human being they could have been without intense therapy. The people that say, "Our parents spanked us, and we turned out okay, didn't we?" do not really want people to respond to that statement.

The adults of my era aren't too different. They have moved away from spanking because you can literally get in more trouble for doing it. Some have realized, it's not that effective overall, just for the moment. But most adults eventually find themselves using shame to control their children. In practice, it's not particularly different. It works to control people quite well for the immediate situation; but it creates all kinds of problems down the road. Shaming children may gain control of the classroom, but the students are wounded afterwards. In my estimation, that's not a workable solution for the long term.

In Junior High, my teachers could spank me and shame me. They did both with a lot of enthusiasm. It controlled me for a little while, but overall, it just made me that much more rebellious. Day by day, I felt dirtier and "sinful." My view of God was also slipping into a God that was just disappointed in me, and really just wanted me to write sentences on the chalkboard so he didn't have to punish me more sternly. In His eyes, what I really deserved was much worse, and I knew this because it was reinforced "religiously."

Nothing in my life really motivated me to find my voice. A couple of times when I found my voice, I got my mouth washed out with soap. The adults in my life generally didn't care what I had to say. Everything I did seemed to disappoint God, so I was sure He didn't care what I had to say. And there were consequences when we talked too much in class, or spoke our mind, or even when we had the wrong look on our face. The first teacher I remember that listened to me was our English teacher, Ms. Allen, who taught me how to write creatively. But that was in high school, and by then my voice was pretty far down in my shadow.

Most of the other systems I grew up in were also religious. Religion is often very shame based. It's different from people that make fun of you. Religion doesn't overtly call you names, or does it? Religion usually sets up the premise that we are pretty *worthless* without whatever solution it is offering. When even my righteous acts are considered *filthy rags* and I'm labeled as a *sinner* and a *wretch* who falls short of the mark, it's hard to gain a lot of confidence, even if someone did redeem me. Because, as Laura implied, there is still a God out there that's an asshole, and it's my fault that he is that way. I mean, they let me say a testimony about how God saved me from all that, but it's hard to feel it deep down when you keep getting pounded every week with the negative side of it. In that system, what do I really have to say? "I'm lucky?"

Christianity is my background, so it is what I can speak to. Most religions have an unspoken rule that it's better if we stay kind of homogenous in our religious tribes, and Christianity is no exception. Isn't that what belief statements are all about? If we are going to be a group, we need to agree to believe mostly in the same things. We have to stay somewhat alike, or they won't know how to recognize us, not to mention that there might be some type of divine retribution when we don't operate under the umbrella of that group's manifesto. One of the problems is that there are between 9,000 and 33,000 protestant denominations worldwide, each with their own system of keeping people the same—see the problem? My point is that it doesn't promote people having a unique voice and usually you get punished for it in one way or another.

The first type of retribution is *rejection.* A few years ago, when I changed some of my beliefs, most of my friends stopped talking to me. A few of them were brave enough to discuss it somewhat online. The number of things we can disagree on are exactly two. They usually argue for a while about the one issue, then they say something like "Let me get this straight Karl. You don't believe in this issue (the way I do) *and* you don't believe in this other issue (the way I do)?" I know when they say that we are just about done. I am about to be shunned. Most times, I don't even get to talk to them, so I admire the ones that do take the time to make the call that I'm a heretic.

Even though most religious people won't admit it, they are apt to respond to differing beliefs, and people that find their voice, with *hostility.* I wish I could confirm that this isn't true, but my tribe (the Christians) were often the most combative to those that were upsetting their stability or challenging their beliefs. Why? Because "wrong" beliefs are considered cancer, and cancer has to be treated aggressively. We don't want it affecting the whole *body.* If I wanted to find my voice, it would be okay for me to speak my truth as long as it continues on the correct doctrinal path (this particular one of 9,000 if we just use the small number).

As I said before, it's pretty tough to find your voice as a pastor, even though you get to write and speak all the time. I was thinking, along with a friend of mine, about book sales in my current situation. I said, "If I were in my old denomination, I could sell a lot of books just because I was in that denomination." He reminded me, though, that they would not read what I am writing now, and I wouldn't want to write what they would find as acceptable. I think finding our voice separates us in a way, and probably most of us love our certainty and don't want to get off whatever track we are on. The trouble is that we sacrifice our voice.

I think all of us want to find this unique voice that is us. But how do I find it? It begins with telling ourselves the right things. We won't be motivated to find our voice and express it when we think of ourselves as worthless. I don't agree any more with religious systems that promote the devaluing of any human beings. I also have to get in front of my inner critic and, with compassion, tell him to knock it off.

Finding my voice means understanding deeply who I am. It is not just about what I have to say, it's about my true self hidden deep within me. It's about what little Joey and the much older Karl have to say, but it's also about who they are and what they stand for. It's not about the belief system they were assigned because of their circumstances, and it's not about the practice they stayed in because of shame and other pressures of that system. It's about who they really are and what they have to share with the world, at least for the ones that earn the right to hear it.

It is important for me to remember not to argue with idiots. Just because someone engages me doesn't mean they are ready to hear my truth. If someone provokes me, it may be much better to turn the other cheek and wait until they are ready to hear it. It may be something about where to cast your pearls, but it is mainly about my self-respect for the importance of my voice. It matters and I matter. I want to be truly heard and understood.

I believe I will get unique chances to share my voice, but it's got to be my voice. When I know who I am, I will most likely know what my voice needs to say. But, with a little mindfulness or prayer, or just a little time, I may also be able to discover who my voice was honed for in the first place.

13

# FINDING THE WORD IN THE DESERT

## *Karl*

I used to walk to the pulpit and hold up the Bible and say, "I have nothing of value to say except what is written in this book." I now regret saying that for a variety of reasons that might become apparent if you have read my book, *Apparent Faith*, or heard me speak lately.

Depending on our backgrounds, we attach varying degrees of emphasis to the Bible. This collection of letters and poetry, and various other forms of literature, have been deemed by some to be the "Word of God," even though the Bible itself gives that title to Jesus in the Gospel of John. Some would ignore the Bible completely, but I would agree with Paul (very simply) that the Bible is "beneficial."[16] I also believe that it is "inspired," but I find no evidence to suggest that it is infallible. Brian Zahnd suggests that Christianity is like a tree

**16** 2 Timothy 3:16

that grows out of the soil[17] of Scripture. Pete Enns points to Walter Bruggemann's characterization of Scripture as compost[18] for a new life.

These definitions are closer to how Jesus portrayed the *Scriptures*—which at that time was only a collection of scrolls, possibly what we call the *Old Testament*. What did Jesus say?

> "You examine the Scriptures because you think that in them you have eternal life; And it is those very Scriptures that testify about me, yet you are unwilling to come to Me so that you may have life have life." (John 5:39–40)

The life is in Jesus, not necessarily the Scripture. The soil and compost are important, but they only lead to the life that grows out of them.

At the transfiguration of Jesus, he is joined by Moses (representing the law) and Elijah (representing the prophets). Together they represent a good portion of the Old Testament. The most interesting thing about this passage is when God says, "This is my Beloved Son, with whom I am well pleased; *Listen to him!*"[19]

Sometimes the Bible can be confusing, but I do not find Jesus' words to be difficult to understand. They are challenging to live by but quite easy to comprehend. He says:

- Love God
- Love your neighbor
- Love your enemy

---

**17** https://brianzahnd.com/2017/08/christianity-tree-growing-soil-scripture/

**18** https://peteenns.com/the-bible-cookbook-or-compost-pile/

**19** Matthew 17:5

- Do to others what you would want them to do to you
- Turn the other cheek

His life demonstrated things like compassion, love, mercy, and grace. These are the things that bring life! When I live this way, life is not hard to understand.

I no longer treat the Bible as an idol. It is useful and I am thankful for it because it points me to Jesus! And Jesus points me to life!

## *Laura*

I grew up Lutheran, which is steeped in tradition. We were in church every Sunday. I distinctly remember sitting in the pews, singing hymns, and listening to the minister take a sentence or two of scripture and create an entire sermon around it. This was my routine for many, many years. I never gave it much thought. Once Karl and I got married and began to attend Baptist churches, I noticed something strange: Everyone brought their Bible to church with them. Not only that, but they also even opened them up and followed along with the pastor. Some of them actually wrote in their Bibles! These were two vastly separate ways to view the Bible.

There are probably two main reasons I currently shy away from the Bible as any part of my spiritual journey: The first reason is because, while I went from literally never being expected to read or carry a Bible into church to being expected to do both, I was never taught how to read the Bible. This enormously daunting book that supposedly holds all the mysteries of God and the universe was simply handed to me without any instructions on how to read it or dissect it. Nothing. I did my best by downloading Bible apps, trying to follow a "Read the Bible in a Year" program, and going to countless Bible studies.

However, this still didn't help me know how to read my Bible. Something that you may not know about me is I struggle with sensory overload—any kind of sensory overload. If the TV is playing and Karl is listening to a podcast: sensory overload. If I have music playing in the car and my oil light continually dings also, sensory overload. Give me a large book with sixty-six chapters, an average of 1,200 pages, and 783,137 words: again, sensory overload. When I experience sensory overload, I shut down. If it's too much, I completely ignore it. That is exactly what happened with my relationship with the Bible.

The second reason my journey with the Bible is struggling is because, in my experience, it has typically been used to spiritually avoid situations or weaponized to achieve our own means. Using it in these ways, we have become experts at using Scripture to set the stage. When people are in crisis, it is easier to quote Scripture than to do the challenging work of sitting with them in their pain.

> "Do not be anxious about anything, but in everything by prayer and pleading with thanksgiving let your requests be made known to God." (Philippians 4:6)

> "There is an appointed time for everything. And there is a time for every matter under heaven." (Ecclesiastes 3:1)

> "Be strong and courageous, do not be afraid or in dread of them, for the Lord your God is the One who is going with you. He will not desert you or abandon you." (Deuteronomy 31:6)

There was definitely a time in my life when these and other verses would give me comfort and, while I am not trying to sound arrogant, I think that time when I could find comfort in these verses was when I was an "immature" believer. What I mean by immature is a time in my spiritual journey when I didn't question anything, so I just took these verses at face value. As Karl and I dug deeper into our 20 years of ministry, there were some real hurts and wounds that I was experiencing (inflicted by people in the church, no less). Not only did these verses not help, but they left me doubting, and doubt was not allowed in the churches we attended. These verses would "bypass" the truth of my spiritual wounds. I learned quickly that it was much easier for others to hand me a verse than to sit with me in my pain.

To be fair, I did the same exact thing when others would come to me in pain. I just think it's what we think at the time is the right thing to do but using scripture this way stops wounded people in their tracks. It is a bandage that keeps the wounded from bleeding all over us and making us uncomfortable. Inevitably, the wounded person begins to question their spirituality. For me, these verses only made me feel more inadequate than I already felt. I mean, I *was* anxious! I *didn't*, not even one percent, feel strong or courageous! I couldn't even pray! Put all those elements together and it is a recipe for sensory overload, which means I shut down.

Today, as of this writing, I still have not picked up the Bible to read it. I have no emotion toward this book, and I refuse to beat myself up over it. Maybe, one day I will find a way to read this text and see it as a love letter or a history book or maybe something else. Right now, I am okay with where I am. I have grace enough for myself to know that whether I open my Bible today, tomorrow, or never, I can still hear the Divine speak truth through many ways other than an ancient book. At this moment, that is enough for me.

## 14

# FINDING NEW PRACTICES IN THE DESERT

### *Karl*

Early on in my reintroduction into religion, I taught junior high Sunday School classes. Not sure why I was qualified to teach them, but with that age group you mostly just have to be willing. They were extremely uncomfortable talking about things like love, but they did have a standard answer for just about everything. It was, "pray, read your Bible and go to church." In their minds, this was the standard answer to just about everything. But why did they think that?

The boys had all been raised in the same type of tradition. This tradition stresses that most problems can be overcome if you will just devote more effort to:

- Having a daily quiet time where you read and meditate on Scripture
- Praying for others and praying for yourself on a regular basis and having faith

- Attending church regularly

Even when I was trained in spiritual leadership coaching in this tradition because we all had the same formation, we still produced these same general conclusions about what our practice should be. We believed that when you were unsure, the best course was to get back to the basics and just keep doing them. But what happens when these practices don't serve us as well as they did in the past? What if they become more constricting than freeing? What happens when we know for sure that we shouldn't go to church right now, and that the Bible is something different than what we originally imagined? For some of us prayer has become more contemplative and less petitionary, and it is so different than it used to be. What is the right way forward?

One of the things I refuse to do is to tell you what your practices should be. Even between Laura and I, different practices feed our soul. There is not one prescription for all people. But there are some principles that will help us along in the journey.

## FEELING GUILTY

When we stopped going to church on Sunday, I felt like I was doing something wrong. We had gone to church consistently for several decades. It was our practice! But, when it didn't work for us, it took a while not to feel guilty about not practicing the same way. It didn't help when some people tossed a little shame our way by stressing "all" should be doing what they are doing. It is unproductive to feel guilty about not practicing like we used to. If it is right for us, we will miss it, and a little time might be the best thing to help us sort it out.

Recently we interviewed Cindy Wang Brandt on our podcast, The Desert Sanctuary. She stressed that most people should take a "gap year" at some point to get away from the practice of going to a church, even if they love going to church. If going to an organized church is right for us, then it should be okay for us to step away for a period. If it's not okay to step away for a time, maybe we should ask why we can't take a break. If it really is what is best for us to practice, it should be okay to take a break and the people there should support us taking time off and welcome us back if we return. As with many other things, it's not a good practice to respond to fear with shaming. Love should allow people the time to do what they need to do.

## DOING NOTHING IS A PRACTICE

I like the practice of centering prayer. I became aware of it through Thomas Keating's book, "Open Mind, Open Heart." By focusing on a sacred word and clearing the mind of all the things that clutter it, we can revive this ancient practice. The beauty of it is that there is nothing to recite or memorize or do. It is simply being still. We don't have to ask for anything or expect anything, and we don't have to feel guilty if we don't do it right, or even if we don't do it at all.

I find myself doing more things like this these days. I find myself just being present and being still more often. When I meditate or close my eyes or take a nap, I feel some of the clutter of my day melt away and I'm able to process the world more clearly. I don't feel guilty like I wasted the time, and I am able to process my world more genuinely when I can take some time to do *nothing*.

## LEARNING FROM OTHERS

One of the best things I get to do these days is podcasts. At first, I felt very awkward interviewing people. Over time, I was able to relax and breathe and just let people talk. It is of benefit during a podcast to listen well. I am learning to do this better. My friends, the sisters at Mount St. Scholastica, taught me to listen deeply—to listen to the heart. Now that I am learning to do this, I draw especially close to people when I listen to them for 45 minutes.

Listening to people helps us understand that practices are somewhat nuanced. When I listen to people, I come to understand not just the practice and what they do, but also the attitude they bring to their practice. How we view the practice, and our world, helps us benefit from what we do when we practice. I love yoga but I don't do it every day. My practice serves me more than I serve it. I don't want to become a slave to the practice, but I want it to help me navigate the human experience better. To understand this, it helps to hear the stories of others.

## SOME STRUCTURE CAN BE HELPFUL

It may be helpful to add some structure (liturgy) to our practices. By borrowing well-crafted prayers from the past and liturgies of other people, we have a place to start and a structure to guide us. If we choose, we can add it to our practice or just leave it behind later.

It is also important to keep stressing that my practices are not a job that I "punch into" every day. It's okay if I miss doing them or do them at a different time. Too often, shame and fear drive everything about our practices. These days, the best thing about my practices is that I do them when I feel like I need to. A little structure helps get me started.

## THE TORTOISE ALWAYS WINS

Last week I realized I had been focused on a specific mantra for several weeks. I'm not in a hurry anymore. I don't have to read the Bible in a specific time frame, or do a quiet time every day, or get an award for going to Sunday School every week. This is my practice, and I can take my time interacting with the deeper places within me.

We have access to so much information. I can watch several powerful sermons in a day on the internet. I can download the best prayers ever written in a matter of seconds. I could literally read almost any book in the world without leaving my chair. I could process and analyze more information daily than ever before. But what I am doing with every practice I have is that I am doing all of them a lot more slowly. The bonus: the practices themselves help me clear my mind and breathe better and focus on what's important, instead of what seems urgent.

## DON'T LOOK FOR PEOPLE TO APPROVE

When I became a vegan, most of the people around me didn't understand and were threatened when I started talking about it. If I was telling them about what was benefiting me, it sounded to them like I was criticizing what they were doing. I take part of the blame for them feeling that way. But any time I say something is right, I cannot necessarily say it is right for everyone, and I shouldn't expect them to patently approve of what I am doing. They either aren't ready for what I am telling them, or it might not be the right practice for them or (gasp) I may be wrong!

Now that I have left my old denomination, I can't expect them to agree with my decisions to change my practices. They simply are in a different place like I used to be. When we stopped going to church, I wanted to talk about it. I wanted to find some answers, but the people that were still going to church weren't as eager to discuss it. They were a little defensive and accused me of bashing the church. I really shouldn't have assumed they would understand. They were still going to church, a decision they obviously think is right. I can't expect them to understand right now.

### THE GAME

One of the things my coaches always stressed in athletics was that how we practiced would be synonymous with how we played the game. It's important to practice because we develop rhythms and patterns. Our minds and our muscles are literally trained to respond to situations and then, when we encounter something in the game, we respond based on how we practiced. If we practice well, we will perform well in the game. I think that's important to remember in our spiritual practice. It's important to practice, and practice well, and often. But the purpose of the practice is to play the game!

Practice, if done right, becomes part of our daily life. We respond and act the same way we practiced. If we are present in our practice, we can be present in daily life. If we are at peace in Centering Prayer, we have a better chance of being at peace when unexpected situations prevail against us. My practices are different now, and it affects how I play the game.

## *Laura*

I remember when Karl first asked me the question, "What are your practices?" It was while we were doing a podcast together on *The Desert Sanctuary*. I was taken back. Practices? I don't have any practice now that we don't go to church! So, that is the answer I gave. I remember him asking, "Is it ok that you don't have any practices?" I wasn't sure how to answer. I didn't know if it was ok or not, but I did know that was where I was at that specific time. Since that podcast, I have had some time to chew on this question and here is what I now know.

## LEAVING CHURCH

I'm starting off with a bang! Usually when people write, they leave the biggest shocker for last. I am starting with this one because, in all honesty, everything else I am now practicing is a result of leaving the institutional organization called the church. I'm speaking of the building, not the people. I get that the church is not just a brick and mortar building and that it is made up of living, breathing people. However, going inside those walls became very painful for me. Being in the ministry had already brought pain into my life, as we've discussed, and continuing to go to a place where my wounds were initiated only kept them from healing.

As much as I didn't want to, when I walked through the doors of the church, I slapped a smile on my face and pretended nothing was wrong. Going to church brought on a level of anxiety that never ended well. When Karl stepped down from our last church, we took maybe two weeks off, but then we started going to a large church about an hour from our small town. I felt a sense of dread the moment my alarm went off. It was the feeling of going through the motions. I had no idea *why* we had to go to church. This feeling only grew as we drove an hour to the church service.

I hadn't found my voice yet, or at least a coherent sentence to express how I was feeling, so the drive there was mostly silent. Karl was excited to be going, to hear the Word, and to sing praise music—a part that I had not enjoyed for a while. He was excited to talk to the pastor, to make connections, to find community. I, however, just wanted to get in, do our "church thing," and get out. It was almost like shopping is for my husband.

I did try to make connections, but remember, church for me was an open wound. I wasn't sure who I could ultimately trust, so the connection was surface level at best. Then came the ride home.

Thinking about it now is still emotional. Like I said, Karl was receiving what he needed. I was wondering "Why the hell do we have to be here?" So, heading home, I would try to find the words to express my anxiety. This only frustrated Karl who was coming off a spiritual high. I brought him crashing down every Sunday as we drove home. Remember how I said it was quiet *going* to church? Well, it was not only quiet coming home from church, but it was also based on anger now. He was irritated with me for, in my opinion, not finding joy in church any longer, and I was mad and resentful because he didn't understand, and I felt like a 5-year-old child who was made to go.

Not knowing how to communicate either of our points to one another at that part of our journey made for Sundays that were more like hell than heaven. Eventually, this tension, mixed with other variables, led to one of the most painful arguments of our marriage. It almost makes me cry thinking about it. Karl had lots of shadow stuff going on, which is his story to tell, but I remember he was being very cold and hurtful one night. I remember I was sobbing on the floor, feeling very much like a little girl who had no voice. Even when I did try to articulate what I wanted to say, it rambled and it was met with sternness, and what felt like an unloving nature from Karl.

The next day he told me he was leaving for a week to talk to some spiritual advisors. This was so painful, but it needed to happen. We had been wounded in separate ways through our 20+ years of ministry and the organizational church, and neither of us had dealt with it. When you don't deal with your stuff, it can come out sideways. This wasn't even sideways, it was a full—blown explosion, and it rocked our world and started to dismantle everything we knew to be true. After this experience, I can honestly say that true healing started to happen in our marriage for the very first time.

Karl continued to go to church, but he completely honored the fact that I couldn't go. I can't say that I do anything special on Sunday mornings now that I don't get ready for church, but there is a sacredness in putting on my leggings and a sweatshirt, listening to a book or podcast, writing a chapter or two in a book I never expected to write, and giving myself a chance to recognize that I do have practices outside of the walls of the church. They are valid and they bring me one step closer to the Divine.

## LOVE

I know, I know, it sounds super trite. I've always thought of myself as a "loving" person, full of compassion. That is partly true. I was loving and compassionate, but mostly toward the people the church deemed worthy. I had even been known to say damaging things like "Hate the sin, love the sinner." Cringe worthy, I know. So, when it came to people who were gay, or who had an abortion, I could love them, but from a distance. In reality, I wasn't loving them as much as I was judging them.

The thing that didn't sit right with me was that I knew people who were in the LGBTQ+ community, and I knew people that had had an abortion. When I say I "knew" them, I mean they were actively part of my life. I was around them. Nothing in me would want to separate myself from them. This was a struggle to reconcile. The church was telling me these things, among others, were sin and I should not associate with them, but love and compassion were telling me something else. Since the beginning of my relationship with the institutional church, I have learned that love was never meant to be held hostage to a list of demands.

My eyes were opened to this two and a half years ago when our first granddaughter, Hollyn, was born. As I mentioned above, I put her ear to my heart, and it was as if no one else was in the room with us. In that moment, the Divine spoke through that baby girl, "This. This right here. This is how I love you. This is how you love others." That was the beginning of my deconstruction. My heart has never been the same since that day. Hollyn had done nothing except exist in that moment. She was, and so I loved her. We muddy the waters when we make loving others anything else. We weaken it when we hold it hostage to a list of demands. And we further diminish its potential when we try to fix and solve and orchestrate.

## PRAYER

If Hollyn taught me about genuine love, Jackson, our grandson, has taught me about prayer. Jackson had contracted a virus in utero called Cytomegalovirus, or CMV, for short. While it is quite common, I had never heard of it. Normally, we all have contracted CMV in our lifetime. Symptoms are feeling like you have a bad cold. The thing is, outside of the womb we can fight it off. When CMV happens in utero, it can create major complications, such as blindness, deafness, premature birth, and cerebral palsy.

My heart sank at this news. I didn't know how to respond. I remember that I just listened. I never once said, "I'll pray." The truth is, I had no idea how to pray about this. I had no words. I couldn't pray because I was angry. I couldn't pray because I was scared. But I also couldn't pray because nothing I had learned about prayer up until this very day seemed adequate.

I wrestled with what would happen if I didn't say the right words and Jackson wasn't "healed." I struggled with how much I should pray, and if I didn't pray this ambiguous number of times that I thought God wanted me to, it would be my fault if Jackson was not "healed." It still amazes me how much I thought Jackson's outcome was dependent on me, however, that is the message we have been engrained with when it comes to prayer.

I must be honest and tell you that I didn't pray in any of those ways when it came to Jackson. When it comes to prayer, Jackson has taught me that being present with people is a form of prayer and is probably most important. Sitting with them in their joys and in their pain and just being. Not fixing or solving. Not offering anything more than fierce listening, a gentle touch, and a box of Kleenex to wipe away much needed tears.

Karl and I both understand prayer to be a connection: connection to the Divine and connection to other people. In any relationship, the need to reach out and connect is the most important aspect of the relationship. It's not what we say as much as extending our gaze and our attention to the ones that matter most to us.

Hollyn had ripped open my heart to the love of the Divine living in me. Jackson helped me realize that prayer is my new heart aligning with the Divine as we wrestle through life together.

15

# FINDING COMPANIONSHIP IN THE DESERT

## *Karl*

I still remember the day my friend Kathy suggested that we call our spiritual direction group "Contemplative Companions." To be brutally honest, I thought the title sounded stupid. To my logical mind it sounded a little juvenile or maybe a little too "girly," if I can say that without being sexist or condescending. Kathy and I were in the same spiritual formation group called Souljourners, where we practiced group spiritual direction, focusing, and deep listening. She was ahead of me in the training, and I trusted her wisdom, I just didn't like the name. But, over time, as I heard the term used more often, it kind of grew on me and it made perfect sense.

Most of the places I have worked in the past 35 to 40 years have had communication problems. If I had to identify the most common issue in my marriage, it would probably revolve around communication. It happens in church, in our civic clubs, and at our family reunions—bad communication! Communication is so important, but often neglected. Often, we take classes in how to speak more eloquently and effectively, but the most pressing aspect of communication is listening.

## TWO TYPES OF LISTENING

If you will allow me to simplify, I will generally divide listening into two major categories: cerebral and contemplative. As a former pastor, I like to illiterate whenever I can, which means to make the main ideas start with the same letter. So, let's start with the *cerebral* listeners, which are usually the most common type in churches. We are ushered into an auditorium where we are invited to listen. But what type of listening are we invited to do? In the old days, they handed us outlines, so we could follow along. Today, we are shown power points to keep us on point and so that we can grasp the main ideas. In this style of listening, we are not listening for the heart, we are striving to *understand* what the speaker is saying so that we can respond to it, either in actions, or sometimes further questions.

In a conversation, when we are listening cerebrally, our minds frantically search for a response to the speaker. Our mind says, "I want to solve your problems and resolve this quickly." In a speech, we talk about takeaways and bullet points. When we hear a lecture, we are encouraged to process it quickly and ask questions. We are rewarded for insightful follow up questions—this is how we gain status. Even in small group Bible studies, when someone shares a problem or issue in their life, we rush to solutions for them or feel remorse that we have no answers for them. Many times, the crosstalk in small groups simply derails good listening because we are listening for an answer rather than really hearing the problem or issue.

In religious circles, this often leads to bypassing. We say things like, "Well, God has a purpose," or "We will understand it better later," or "You will get through this," or some other placating statement to defuse our level of displeasure with being uncomfortable.

The trouble with cerebral listening is we usually are not really listening. We identify a familiar idea or concept and begin formulating our next response before the person even finishes telling us about their feelings, or discouragement, or questions. Somehow, we have to learn to get out of our head and listen with our heart. That is what my contemplative companions are teaching me.

## CONTEMPLATIVE LISTENING

Contemplative listening is more about being in the present moment without judgment or any attempt to change it. Because of a belief that God is present in every moment, this evocative approach attempts to help the speaker identify and name their present inner experiences and find meaning for themselves. When people have listened to me in this way, it seems more like they are groaning or experiencing this with me. It is the good kind of groaning where I sense they are feeling what I feel. I feel like we are on a journey together to reveal what is inside me and respond to the Divine in that situation.

Contemplative, evocative listeners use several methods like determined silence, savoring, reflecting, summarizing, and clarifying to help the speaker discover their own inner wisdom. Questions are always open ended so that the listener is not leading the speaker, and usually focused on understanding better the heart of the speaker. In my opinion, another necessary quality or skill is that the listener must listen with *eyes of grace*. The speaker must be able to see that the listener is understanding, but not judging or trying to "fix" them.

Deep listening truly helps us find in our bodies where we are storing our trauma. I am really not qualified to explain this fully but let me briefly share my experience. When we are able to identify the main issue and where we feel it in our bodies, we are more apt to visit that issue in a caring way. Spiritual directors are skilled at *focusing* and helping people to explore this extremely helpful process. I always come away from a focusing session feeling like I've touched a deep part of myself, and that I have listened with compassion to what it has to teach me. I encourage you to investigate further.

To me, the bottom line is that this effective type of listening helps us access the Divine and see more clearly where we are hurting and how we can move forward. My hope is that everyone will find some contemplative companions who can listen to them deeply. I pray that this process touches your heart and soul, instead of just satisfying you intellectually.

## MINDFULNESS

When I went through deconstruction, a couple of the first things I was scolded for was meditation and yoga. After four years of experimenting with both, I have never experienced anything troubling, and I never slid down the slippery slope people said I was on. I have only positive things to say, and I genuinely believe mindfulness to be one of my most vital and important practices. Especially in listening, it is particularly important for me to compassionately dismiss my many anxious thoughts (sometimes known as the "monkey mind") so that I can listen effectively. My only regret about mindfulness is that I haven't had it as a tool for the whole first half of my life.

Mindfulness helps us get past all the watchful dragons and chaotic thoughts that cloud our minds. Watchful dragons are defense systems that keep us from going deeper. Being a contemplative listener demands an intentional process, or preparation, to hear nothing but the speaker and their encounter with the Divine. I don't have time to deal with all the objections to meditation and mindfulness. All I can offer you is my testimony that it helps me listen much more effectively when my mind is focused and alert. And mindfulness makes that possible.

So, why am I talking about contemplative listening in a book about organized religion? I'm glad you asked. If we think about it carefully, most organized religion doesn't have the time, patience, or inclination to listen effectively. In our minds, we want to listen to others and reap the benefits from it, but we can't imagine—in our minds—spending that much time preparing to listen and being disciplined enough to truly hear people and listen evocatively. The church is busy doing cerebral things because it is how we imagine discipleship playing out.

In my opinion, the church would be much better served hosting a contemplative retreat than another 12-week study to "understand" better cerebrally. We would be much healthier with Holy Listening groups than small groups to help us fix each other. In all of our groups, we must learn to listen better and hear each other more deeply. This is most effectively done contemplatively.

## SOME OF MY COMPANIONS

The list of my contemplative companions grows larger every day. I'm an introvert, but I can't tell you how much I appreciate these people in my life.

As I mentioned before, Kathy has been instrumental in my contemplative growth. She has set a consistent example for me to follow and given timely guidance through sharing her journey with many of us.

Sister Marcia, my spiritual director for about a year, also led me to understand how to listen and focus, and truly hear people as they interact with the Divine in them. The word companion sounds a lot like "friend," and I am so thankful for this friend that breaks many of my previous paradigms and has taught me so much.

My wife, Laura, is a natural contemplative listener. She doesn't even understand how it works or even exactly what it is, but she has always been one of the best listeners I know and a natural at contemplative life. She also asks the best questions—she always has!

Dr. Paul is a companion that has always been a part of my journey (at least for the past 20 years or so). I message him at all hours of the day, and he is always there. He doesn't lecture me or try to fix me, but he always has something that I need to hear. But the best part about this companion is that he always seems to understand my issues, because he is a good listener. His only equal is his wife, Susanna. The Fitzgerald's have taught me to always stretch forward while pausing occasionally to do the inner work.

Another interesting companion in my life are the podcasters I know online. They are the new radio hosts of the present age. The dozen or so contemplative listeners that host my favorite podcasts can be identified by their response to their interviewees. Some of them might not identify as contemplatives, but they are contemplative listeners, just the same. You can most often hear them in the background saying something that sounds like groaning. Their response is more like feeling what is said, their follow up questions are clarifying more than leading, and their overall response is to promote the guest rather than interject their own opinion. More often than not, I love listening to podcasts where the host is a good listener.

I don't think the phrase "contemplative companions" is dumb anymore—I think it's a good explanation of what these people are.

They are not coaches, they are different than counselors, and they are better than average friends. They help me experience something deeper than the cerebral—they help me interact with the Divine. They touch my heart.

It may sound pedestrian, but I can't imagine my life without my contemplative companions. I pray that you find yours.

## *Laura*

Social media is both a blessing and a curse. It is a blessing of sorts because it is a way to connect with people from our lives currently, as well as from our past. I still have a childhood friend that I stay connected with through Facebook, as well as a high school friend, and friends from various places that we have lived. I am able to see how their children are growing, where they are vacationing, and all the other milestones of life that they want to share with me and their Facebook world.

However, as I think about the prevalence of social media, I can't help thinking about its downside. Many times, we see it as a means of connection with people, however, most times that connection is superficial. We show the best parts of our lives on social media, or at least I do! I want people to have this (sometimes unrealistic) expectation that my life is all butterflies and unicorns. Some days what I wouldn't do for a unicorn!

When you are deconstructing and leaving some very real, very secure things behind—your church, your beliefs, your certainty about anything and everything—you find out who your devoted friends are. When we began to question everything, people we thought were friends, people who said, "You are my best friend!" (Even though we only knew each other for a couple of years), began to drop like flies.

When that happens, it is common to question your own sanity. If you weren't already in the desert, having those you thought were your friends literally abandon you will thrust you into it, and you'll find yourself face down in the sand hoping someone, anyone, will hand you a glass of water.

As I continue to evolve, I am finding there is a difference between friends and companions. For me, friends are those I call to do things like go to the movies, get our nails done, or grab some breakfast on a Saturday morning. Friendships can be long lasting, but typically our level of conversation is around what we have in common and, if I don't overstep those boundaries, our friendship can remain intact. There is nothing inherently wrong with that. We all need people in our lives with whom we can share a laugh, some tasty food, and a much-needed pedicure.

These times with my friends are treasured, and I definitely leave our time together with a smile on my face. However, when I was in the depths of my deconstruction, it was hard to be transparent with my friends. Telling my friends that I was questioning everything put a major awkward factor into our relationship. They became extremely concerned about my eternal wellbeing. I quickly learned it was best not to discuss these things for the sake of our friendship. In addition, as a pastor's wife, I could not speak of such things with the "friends" I had at church. That would have absolutely wrecked the fabric of church life if the pastor's wife was questioning the very essence of doctrine, church, and religiosity.

Companionship is something quite different altogether. A companion is one who travels with you on your journey. The two of us do not have to agree on everything or even always be going to the same destination, but we can honor one another for where we are in our individual journeys.

Since arriving in the desert, I have found people that will travel this journey with me. First, Karl. It has taken us some time to get to this point, but we are finally at a place where we can honor each other's journeys. We are not in the same place spiritually, and while that terrified me at first, his words of "It's ok to be where you are and who you are," have given me great peace as I am finding the truth that I can own.

I still look at him in amazement sometimes when he says these words. In all honesty, those words may have always been there for me, but indoctrination told me that I had to believe what he believed. Our desert journey has allowed us to commune in our companionship and honor where we are at this very moment, not worrying about where we will be tomorrow.

My children are some of my greatest companions. I know this can sound strange, but I have never wanted to be my children's best friend, or even just their friend. When they were young, I was too busy being their "mom" to be their "friend." I'd like to think they were grateful for that. However, as they have grown up and started their own lives and families, the label of "friend" never stuck. It didn't seem right. Yet, when I think of the word companion, that word settles on what we have together as something genuine.

I want to journey with them as they navigate marriage, children, and their jobs. I want them to know that I see them, and I hear them, and that I honor them as I walk beside them. I want them to know that I feel the same from them. When we began our journey into this vast desert wilderness, Karl took our girls and their husbands out on the porch to talk to them. He thought he was going to break some monumental news to them, and maybe if they were outside, they wouldn't make a huge scene and scare the neighbors? What he found, what we found, was their companionship. We saw it in their eyes,

"We've been waiting for you." This brings tears to my eyes even as I write about it. Companionship says, "I see and honor where you are right now. I may not agree, but we can still love and respect each other on this journey." When our girls communicated this to Karl, it was as if they had said they already deeply understood this. To this day, I am grateful to call all three of my children my companions on this journey. For me, that is so much greater than friendship.

I have also found such loving companions from the most unorthodox places. I have found a beautiful podcast community. We don't always agree, but that space is safe, and it is sacred. I have been able to, over time, share my heart, find my voice, and speak my truth. Some days are easier than others, but on those days where it is not easy, there is grace.

There are also those whom I have found that are questioning like me. They have been in church all their lives, but things are shifting, and now they have questions. They can no longer believe in the things of their youth. As I have shared in the safe spaces, people I know, people that I would have never guessed were questioning, have found me, and said, "me too." I am grateful to offer them a place to be heard and to quietly listen.

What I hope to keep saying to them is, "I hear you; I see you, and what you are feeling is valid." I want to encourage them to be brave as they enter this desert wilderness. I want them to know that they will find companionship here!

16

# FINDING UNCERTAINTY IN THE DESERT

## *Karl*

For over 20 years, I held my theology close to my chest. There were some things that were considered *essentials*. I often recited what is usually attributed to Augustine, "In essentials, unity; in nonessentials, liberty; in all things, charity." Essentials are considered by many groups as the things that are written in stone. We don't change them, we don't even discuss them much, and they are the nonnegotiable things about our belief system. I used to encourage people to not argue about them. What I meant was *don't ask questions*!

For my tradition, my people developed *The Baptist Faith and Message*. This document did not always exist. It was originally adopted in 1925, several years after the rise of Fundamentalism in the United States. It was republished in 1963 and, then again, in 2000. So, the document is not infallible, although it claims the Scriptures are, and I have some questions about that. Protestants, in general, despise the hierarchy of the Catholic church. But, when it comes to doctrinal statements, trust me, most mainline denominations are very structured, and questions are discouraged. Only a few duly elected people can tinker around with the doctrinal statement.

Peter Enns describes this need for certainty:

> "Correct thinking provides a sense of certainty. Without it, we fear that faith is on life support at best, dead and buried at worst. And who wants a dead or dying faith? So, this fear of losing a handle on certainty leads to a preoccupation with correct thinking, making sure familiar beliefs are defended and supported at all costs. A faith like that is stressful and tedious to maintain. Moving toward diverse ways of thinking, even just trying it on for a while to see how it fits, is perceived as a compromise to faith, or as giving up on faith altogether. But nothing could be further from the truth. Aligning faith in God and certainty about what we believe and needing to be right in order to maintain a healthy faith—these do not make for a healthy faith in God. In a nutshell, which is the problem. And that is what I mean by the "sin of certainty."[20]

So, several years ago, I started asking questions with the assumption, "maybe I am wrong." What emerged is what I described in my book *Apparent Faith: What Fatherhood Taught Me About the Father's Heart.* It wasn't easy, but it paid beautiful dividends eventually. Later in this book, I take a closer look at the Beatitudes—not to question their validity, but just to ask new questions. I'm not the same person I was 20 years ago, and I can gain fresh insight into their relevance for me today. Right now, let's take a look at a prayer common to many groups these days called *The Jesus Prayer.*

"Lord Jesus Christ, Son of God, have mercy on me, a sinner."

---

**20** Peter Enns, *The Sin of Certainty: Why God Desires Our Trust More Than Our "Correct" Beliefs.* San Francisco: HarperOne, 2016

Let's just ask a few questions. My first question is "where did it originate?" As a formal prayer, its origins are in the Egyptian Desert by the Egyptian Fathers. In the Bible, Luke recounts a parable of Jesus where Jesus encourages the disciples to pray like the publican, "God, be merciful to me, the sinner!"[21] So, this lends credibility to most people. Jesus was a fan of praying for mercy. He said, "I desire compassion, rather than sacrifice."[22] This is actually a quote from the prophet Hosea. But do we need to pray this every day? In another place, the Bible says, His acts of mercy "are new every morning."[23] Do we really have to ask for them, or would a loving God extend that mercy without being asked? Maybe, Jesus was telling the Pharisee that the Publican was discovering the right way to think. Was Jesus simply reinforcing his message that he doesn't require a sacrifice, even to pray—doesn't he give mercy freely?

But I still have more questions about this prayer. My primary question is, "What do I need relief from?" In other words, "Why do I need mercy?" Is God going to punish me for my sins? I am inclined to moving away from the doctrine of eternal conscious torment. I don't even see God generally as retributive because Jesus didn't demonstrate that as a reality of how God works. Jesus wasn't inclined to condemn or punish the people, he had mercy and compassion for them. So, what was He going to do that I didn't want him to do? Can we see why it might be good to ask questions?

This leads me down a different path. If Jesus said that he desired mercy, I would assume that He generally does what He intends to do.

---

**21** Luke 18:13

**22** Matthew 12:7

**23** Lamentations 3:23

So, am I praying that God will do what he already intended to do? If God desires all to be saved (delivered), I will assume that, eventually, He is going to do that. Yes, I said it! If He desires to exhibit mercy toward me, does it make Him more likely to do it because I pray that he does it? Does He need me to be willing for Him to have mercy on me for Him to demonstrate mercy toward me?

For my friends that practice this prayer regularly, please don't interpret this as a criticism. Asking questions does not negate a belief or practice. In reality, it does something different. When we discover a practice or prayer, we receive it with a certain bias. We accept its meaning as whatever our current understanding of it is. Even if it has been practiced for hundreds of years, we begin practicing it just as we understand it today. As our understanding grows, our relationship to the practice or prayer also should mature. To defend vigorously our understanding of the practice, belief, or even Scripture, is to plunge into the certainty that Pete Enns warns against. It can cause us to stagnate and become defensive and doesn't necessarily lead us in the right direction.

My hope is that we will keep asking questions. At first, it can seem like everything is unraveling, but we can't discover the gift inside a package until we unwrap it. Questions help us discover the deeper and fuller parts of everything. The eternal treasure is not at surface level and questions help us mine the depths to find the pure gold of our practice, prayers, and sacred writings.

Asking questions helps us ask better questions. Even after I discover the treasure, I still have more questions. Where did it come from? How was it used? What do I observe about it that I never saw before?

In my opinion, the two-year-old that asks questions should never be dissuaded. Too many impatient parents inadvertently deter their curious toddlers from the path of discovery by demanding they "stop asking questions!" Their subtle assertion is, "I will tell you when there is something you need to know," and that implication gets reverberated throughout their future lives. People tell them what is true, and they repeat it as truth and, like their parents, they get irritated when people ask them clarifying questions. "Why, why, why" becomes an annoying distraction from their love affair with being certain, and they squash any questions that arise. *They* assume, *we know what we believe, and we are persuaded that what we currently assert to be true is as clear as it gets—no questions necessary. Get on board, let's get moving. Stop slowing us down. We aren't due for another doctrinal update for another 20 years. We will let you know when something changes.*

If we really care about what we claim to care about, we should question it!

## *Laura*

I am sure I mentioned my love of all things certain. My belief was that as my certainty would increase, so would my level of security. It has taken me many years to realize that the two do not necessarily go together. The fact is, when I would dig my heels in deep in the name of certainty, anything and everything began to rock that sure foundation.

I have always been quietly inquisitive. By this I mean I would question things, but not aloud. Instead, when a question about God or church would enter my head, I would stuff it down, trying not to give it another thought. When a question or thought did somehow leak out, it would be met with a solid scripture teaching or spiritual bypassing. You know, things like "God is in control." Those things served a purpose for a season—until they no longer did.

Throughout our ministry life, I have led several bible studies, and I have been a member of a few worship teams. I was the pastor's wife, which was one of my jobs. I did find some joy in these activities. It was my way of ministering to the hearts of those present: the hurting, the broken, and the wounded. Through various women's bible studies, I was able to let women know that they were worthy, that they were a child of the King, and that they were a valid, breathing human worthy of love and adoration. The same message was filtered through the words I would help sing on Sunday morning. And when I sang them, I sang them for *you*: the addicted, the uncertain, the questioning. I wanted you to know that you had my permission to be wherever you were. However, in all of this, I forgot to give myself that permission, and all the years of stuffing my uncertainty and my questions down began to come to the surface. This was frightening. I was the pastor's wife. I was supposed to be sure.

Fast forward to that day I held Hollyn only hours after she was born. In that moment I was not sure of anything except for the tremendous love I felt for her, and in that moment, that's all that mattered. The days that followed, however, I describe as a *nervous breakdown*. I do not say that lightly, but I know of no other way to describe it. I cried all the time. I didn't know what to think or what to do. All I wanted was to be with Hollyn—to have our hearts connect in that deeply spiritual way it did back in the hospital room. I believe, in that moment, and maybe for the first time, I encountered the Divine. But there was no fanfare at that moment. There was no order of worship service. There was no one right or wrong. There was no certainty. It was just this moment, and I was in it, and feeling it, and accepting it. It was a moment of presence. All I had to do was be.!

And it shattered my world!

I am now realizing that it's moments like that that must happen—something that shakes the very foundation of certainty so we can come to that place of grace and not knowing. For me that was a very scary place. When everything started to crumble, I remember thinking, "Am I an atheist?" "What do I believe?" "Is there a heaven?" "What about hell?" "Does God really punish His children for eternity?" But my favorite question of all was, "Who is God? Is God a Man, Woman, or a spirit?"

My need for certainty had pushed all of these very real, very valid questions down to the depth of my being. Now, as my world was turned upside down, they were spilling out of me, and it scared me. I literally accepted the possibility that I might go to hell if I died tomorrow.

Let me assure you, dear reader: you are not destined to hell for questioning. In fact, you are so not alone in your questioning. Questions are good!

As a second-grade teacher, one of my responsibilities is to teach students how to ask good questions. In fact, it is one of our standards, so we don't have a choice but to teach them how to ask good, deep, critical questions. We encourage them to wonder daily and to find new ways to explore and find—or not find—the answer. We give them permission to not take things at face value—to find new and unusual ways to solve problems. Then, we walk into church on Sunday, and we are told what to think, how to think, and the encouragement to question is all but stripped away from us. Today, I have more courage to risk; I ask the challenging questions even if they don't have answers now (or ever); and I am living with continual uncertainty. I reserve the right to have unanswered questions.

## 17

# FINDING ACCEPTANCE IN THE DESERT

*"Blessed are the poor in spirit, for theirs is the kingdom of heaven."*

MATTHEW 5:3

### *Karl*

When I started through my deconstruction, I realized that this journey was taking me out into the desert. I knew that I would lose many of my friends. Some of them would be angry with me, others would feel sorry for me, some of them might even be jealous, who knows? One thing is for sure, it got quiet rather quickly. A couple of people stood me up and then many of them just didn't have time to schedule anything with me or call me back.

Later, when I started attending a certain church, some people from a different church had unusual but somewhat expected reactions to my choices. When we decided not to go to church and started just staying home on Sunday, another wave of rejection surfaced when people either shamed us for not being in church, or just stopped talking altogether. It left me wondering whether I truly was accepted by God—his people surely weren't making me feel that way, except when I did what they wanted me to.

I have always loved the Sermon on the Mount. Some say it was a collection of sermons or maybe just the same sermon delivered more than once and summarized. Either way, it is the core of Jesus' teaching on how to live. Some have also described the Sermon on the Mount as *reforming the Torah.* Israel started with twelve tribes–Jesus began with twelve disciples when He set out to reform the world into a new type of kingdom. The Sermon on the Mount is counter-cultural and somewhat revolutionary. One thing is for sure, if the church is going to be viable, Jesus' words and teachings are primary, and the Sermon on the Mount is essential.

But what does it mean to be poor in spirit and who is it that is accepted in the kingdom of heaven?

First of all, *Makarios* which is usually translated *blessed* can mean several things: *blessed, happy, fortunate*, etc. The word I like best is *fortunate*. The person is fortunate who possesses these qualities. Jesus emphasizes the quality of being poor. This word means *destitute, completely lacking resources, helpless as a beggar, lacking, or abject.* So, this fortunate person is completely abject when it comes to spiritual things. See what I mean about countercultural? The Kingdom of Heaven is for that person or those persons.

It might help us understand this passage if we realize who Jesus was talking to. The simple answer is everyone! Jesus was talking to his disciples, but everyone else was listening, indirectly. According to a previous verse (Matthew 4:25), there were people from Galilee, Jerusalem, Judea, the Decapolis (think Gentile), and even beyond the Jordan coming to hear Jesus speak. There were the religious, the disciples, the Gentiles, the losers, and the winners—pretty much all of humanity was represented. This was not just a secret handshake meeting for the disciples.

That is important because when a verse mentions the kingdom of heaven, or Heaven, or eternity, our first question is "who is in?" I believe that's the wrong question. We ask this question because we want to exclude those that don't belong or qualify. We long to know what our tribe needs to do to be in the club—who is God really for?

Just for the sake of simplicity, let's go with that question. Now that we've wandered out into the desert, now more than ever, we want to know if we are accepted. The first group of people to consider are those that don't know. Wouldn't those that are excluded, left out, or ignored be considered poor in spirit? What about those that are mentally incapable or limited, would they be considered poor in spirit? The Kingdom of Heaven is for people like them.

The second group of people to consider might be the bad people. Every tribe and nation have a unique way to identify the bad people. Have you ever considered that those we call "bad guys" probably use similar adjectives to describe us? We are the "bad guys" to them. We could get super spiritual and start listing our criteria that we use to determine who is the worst, but honestly, it is usually just a bias that works in our favor. We're all bad in someone's eyes! Jesus didn't exclude the "bad" people—He sought them out (think demoniac). He didn't bunker down and throw stones at them—He went to them and showed us that the kingdom of heaven is for those types of people–the poor in spirit.

Another group that is much more acceptable to religious tribes are the humble. This is an easy one because we all know that God honors the humble. We know that when we are humble, God lifts us up (exalts us). This is the easiest category of people to accept as being in the club because they are voluntarily choosing to be humble. That is so honorable, and at the same time, so hard to do! They are poor in spirit, voluntarily. This leads me to the next group.

The Bible also tells us that when we are prideful, God inevitably humbles us. I often wonder if it matters how I get there—I mean, I know it's probably less painful to go voluntarily, but it seems that God gets us there one way or another. Even when we are confused about our status and think we are "rich" and "need nothing," the book of Revelation states that our true situation is "wretched, miserable, poor, blind and naked."[24] There is that word again: poor! Even the proud and confused are poor in spirit.

The last group that I want to consider are those who are not on the inside–those in different tribes. We should be careful with our nationalism. In the United States, we are so patriotic that we often associate our spirituality with our politics and pride for our nation. God does not have special fondness for Americans over any other nation. He is especially fond of all nations, creeds, tribes, and people groups. In a sense, they are all the same kind of poor.

Whatever our formula for separating ourselves, it is usually self-serving and biased. In many ways, maybe the poor in spirit are all of us. God is for us—all of us! Isn't that at least part of the good news?

*God is all in! I think it's most important that we understand we are accepted!*

I would like to give you a step-by-step approach to gain the input you need in your life, but formulas never really work for me. I either bargain with them or forget the equation or just lose interest. It's about a relationship—and relationships are messy and complicated. May I suggest starting over, often by taking enough time to realize

---

**24** Revelation 3:17

that we are accepted, and that God is for us? If Jesus needed that input, I'm sure we do.

Over time, I have been able to feel the acceptance that Jesus was talking about. Sometimes I feel it through my friends. But, most often, it is when I get quiet and still and realize that if God is God and a good father, he must be totally accepting. The "poorest" of us is really all of us, and all are equally accepted just the way we are. We find that the Kingdom of Heaven is ours to discover inside ourselves when we become poor enough in spirit to realize it was always there.

For me, the desert has made this a reality.

## *Laura*

It has taken me a while to begin this part of our book. I have always admired how Karl has been able to look at scripture and glean so much from it. I remember watching him sit for hours, studying scripture, only to be amazed at the words that came out of his mouth from the pulpit on Sunday morning. Surely God was speaking through him. The Divine was indeed speaking through Karl. So, once I started writing this section of our book, the old voices came back, screaming, "You aren't even 1% qualified to talk about Bible stuff! You don't even study it, let alone read it these days!" So, I let those voices silence me for a bit, but I've decided to courageously go where perhaps I am not comfortable going, because that is all part of the process of accepting where I am and where I have been.

I think it has always been easy for me to accept others. My nature is one of compassion. A notable example of my level of compassion is the fierce rivalry we have in our home. He is an Oklahoma Sooners fan; I am a Texas Longhorn fan. If you don't follow college football, this probably means nothing to you. However, if you are a college football fan, you are already cringing and wondering how we have avoided filing for divorce after all these years! We are both diehard fans of our teams, and over the years we have learned to root for each other's teams—as long as they aren't playing each other! Yet, when that Red River Rivalry game is on, it's every person for themselves! We dig our heels in and do our best trash talking for the next three and a half hours. However, Karl will be the first to tell you, even if my Texas Longhorns are winning, when they show the face of a dejected Oklahoma Sooner player, I can't help but feel sorry for them. I stop the trash talking—if only for a moment—and have compassion for them. I've always had a soft spot toward others, and I just do not like to see people hurting.

Our churches have a lot of hurting people. These hurts run a huge spectrum. The thing is many times we go inside the church walls only to find people in their best attire with smiles on their faces. I cannot tell you how many times I was miserable on the drive to church, dragging myself up the church steps dreading every step I took, only to slap a smile on my face once those doors were open. I couldn't let my truth show because, in my experience, it would not be accepted. For goodness' sake, I didn't even accept it!

In the recesses of my mind, it was wrong to be anything but "happy" once I entered the walls of the church. No one was to know my pain—at least not fully know it. There was so much shame around my struggles with religion and church. I was the pastor's wife, so how could I let those struggles be known? If I did, I just knew I would be responsible for single handedly taking my husband's ministry down—at least that is what the voices inside my head were telling me.

When we silence ourselves, when we push our questioning down to the depths, we lose acceptance of ourselves. We find that the place we are in, at that moment, is not valid. We find ourselves in the desert—a place that seems like a vast wasteland. It is dry and lonely. A place where it seems like it is just us—alone. Looking back, I think, for me, this was necessary. For so long, what I had given to others in the form of grace, compassion, and acceptance, I had not made room for within myself.

The desert, as lonely as it was in the beginning, was what I needed. It was a place to reflect. It was a place to sit with myself and grieve, to validate my questioning, my hurts, and my unbelief in many things I once thought were true. It was a place to not accept, as well. It was a place to not accept the voices that told me I wasn't enough: smart enough, biblical enough, godly enough—all of it! The desert is the place where I am, perhaps for the first time in my life, finding not only acceptance for myself and others, but affirmation. I am also finding that there are people in the desert who accept and affirm me in whatever phase of my spiritual evolution I find myself in.

The thing that is mysteriously beautiful about the desert is its vastness. We can travel a great distance before we find an oasis to drink from. But, trust me, we will find it. Along the way, we will see beautiful things because, contrary to what I first believed, there is life in the desert. Things grow and flourish there. There is a vibrant life there, and we know it when we see it thriving. In the desert, it is typically in the cool darkness of the night that things come alive—it's when we least expect it.

When we find living things that honor each other and commune together, we will be glad we stayed on the journey long enough to find this sacred oneness. This genuine acceptance is what we have been looking for all along!

18

# FINDING COMFORT IN THE DESERT

*"Blessed are those who mourn, for they will be comforted."*

MATTHEW 5:4

## *Karl*

I always had a suspicion that the order of things mattered. It seems significant that the first beatitude is about being poor in spirit. I find great comfort that the Kingdom is for normal people, and maybe the first step is realizing that we are accepted. I'm glad that Jesus put that one first. However, I can't say that I am as excited about the second statement.

I've never been a fan of funerals. I don't remember my family being emotional. I know my mother cried—it kind of comes with the territory when you raise four boys. I only went to a couple of funerals in the first 20 years of my life. Suffering, grief, and mourning didn't sound like something I wanted to experience. Until I became a pastor, I pretty much avoided it altogether. However, real comfort generally only comes when we mourn. I started to understand this, like most people, when my Grandpa Joe died.

For the first time, I really allowed myself to feel what it is like to mourn. I had spent every birthday for the first 18 years of my life with him and my grandma. He was one of the most interesting people I knew, and I could truly see the impact he made on people and the void that his death would bring. It personally affected me, and I had to deal with that loss. So, I wrote a poem that I was able to read at the funeral. He was one of those people that had to have their funeral in a gymnasium because of the love people had for him. That was a great tribute, but it just made it harder to process my grief, and I was tempted to fade back into the shadows. I'm glad that I was able to get through it—it helped me greatly.

I always tell people that funerals are not *for* the person that is deceased, but they are *about* them. It's a time to remember and talk about that person, but it doesn't really do them any good. Conversely, funerals and memorials are not about us, but they *are* for us. Jesus decided the second thing he would say in the Sermon on the Mount is that mourning is a good thing—we need it and it's necessary! Yet funerals are not the only place that we mourn. At least a couple of these ideas were nurtured by my good friend, Dr. Paul Fitzgerald.

## THE MISTAKES WE MAKE

This type of mourning begins when we become aware of our shortcomings. Ignorance is bliss, but it usually doesn't lead to healing or anything productive. However, when we humbly acknowledge our mistakes and change our course, make amends, and forgive ourselves, then we can move from our pain and suffering into healthy change. When we acknowledge that what we are doing is ineffective, or admit where we failed, we can find freedom to change our life instead of repeating cycles of denial or self-pity.

The times of notable change in my life have generally been when I allowed myself to truly be sorry for the way I was living. The story that I was telling myself about my life had to be the story that was true. It hurt to see the real me. However, until I faced the painful reality, change was extremely difficult. In a way, I had to die to truly find myself.

### EMPATHY AND LOVE

The way I understand empathy is the term "me too." Shame loves isolation. Dr. Paul Fitzgerald says, "Mourning is sometimes empathy and love that expands to identify with the grief of all humanity and the suffering of others."[25] William P. Young says, "If anything matters, then everything matters."[26] Empathy gets beyond what matters to us and feels the pain and suffering of others. Jesus mourned over people and cities, and even his personal friend.

I am tempted at times to live my life in a bubble. People make things messy. Life is hard; life is painful; people just make it even harder. At those times, I am tempted to just go to work, come home and "mind my own business." Some of us were even taught this as kids. We were told "tend to your own knitting" or "mind your own beeswax" or even just "do your own thing." Real mourning is not just dealing with our personal loss, it is also going outside ourselves to tend to the needs of others.

---

**25** From a personal email while writing this manuscript, November 2020

**26** https://www.goodreads.com/quotes/153155-if-anything-matters-then-everything-matters-because-you-are-important

## PERSONAL LOSS

Over the years, I've tried to figure out what's going on at a funeral. After 20 or so years in ministry, I understand less than I did when I started. There is a deep need to come together and grieve. All of us have different things we want to do at the loss of a loved one, the loss of a job, or even the ending of a relationship. The only thing I know for sure is that if we don't mourn the loss, we will experience repercussions later down the road. If we don't feel the pain of the loss, we will see it in our anger or depression or sadness at a future date when we least expect it. Comfort most often comes from mourning.

Jesus found comfort through his mourning. The church fathers used to say "The unassumed is unhealed."[27] Like Jesus, we must take on the pain of alienation, suffering, or the loss of friends and feel it to find comfort. When Jesus mourned over Jerusalem and Lazarus, He gave us a model of the path to finding comfort. He experienced the feelings. He wept. He found comfort!

Comfort is not excusing the situation or giving patronizing platitudes. Comfort cannot be found in avoiding the pain or even in delaying it. In most cases, we cannot comfort ourselves, but we *will be comforted* when we decide to intentionally mourn.

## STEPS TO COMFORT

Like most things, principles cannot always be reduced to a formula. But here are a few suggestions from a late bloomer in mourning.

We must acknowledge the reality of life that some things about it are difficult. There are things about life that are painful and avoiding

---

27 https://www.apostolictheology.org/2014/12/the-incarnation-unassumed-is-unhealed.html

those things only makes them more complicated and sometimes more painful. It wasn't easy to go to my grandpa's funeral, but it was good!

We should learn to lean into the things that are painful. Regardless of our personality or temperament, eventually we will have to talk about, feel, and process the things that cause us pain. At certain points, we might even need to grasp the reality that it's okay to not be okay for a while, and that, my friends, is painful! Leaning into pain seems wrong at first, but most often pays great dividends.

As we begin to heal, we acknowledge what is changing. Change is not just okay—it is often necessary. Just because things will be different doesn't mean they can't be beautiful. It is important that we embrace necessary change even when we don't fully understand. Maybe, it is like embracing the future instead of clinging to the past. My life is different without my grandpa, but it is still a beautiful life.

Jesus needed to mourn to be comforted. I probably should have just left It there, but I know that all of us try to minimize our experience involving grief and pain. There really are no shortcuts to healing or growth. There are probably a dozen things that I mourn about currently. Be assured that I'm learning to mourn more effectively, and in due process, I'm finding that comfort that Jesus spoke of long ago.

## *Laura*

Mourning—one of my *least* favorite topics. I am by nature a "fixer" which means I don't like to see others in pain, nor do I want to experience it myself. While today I can spot spiritual bypassing a mile away, back in the day I would consider myself an expert at deflecting anything painful and in turn helping others deflect their pain as well by using some oh so quaint statements like, "There's always a silver lining" or "We just aren't meant to understand it all." Gross, right?

If you are reading this and I gave you that bullshit advice, I'm so genuinely sorry. I have learned that you can't avoid pain in life, no matter how hard you run from it or dress it up. It's part of this life and may I say now, after years of reflection and counseling, that it is hard and beautiful. It is both/and.

As I am writing this part of this chapter, it turns out that 2 years have passed since we initially wrote this book. We just noticed that I "conveniently" forgot to add to this chapter. So, here I am, two years later. Maybe it's important that I waited this long. Maybe life had more to teach me about mourning.

On Friday, January 21, 2022, little did I know how mourning would be an integral part of my life. That seems funny to say because I did mourn when we left the church and when I left what I had always known as Christianity. I had to mourn that part of myself that no longer existed. Isn't that what mourning is? We acknowledge that there is a person, a pet, a part of our lives that no longer exist as it was. It's a complete mind shift from what you have always known to the unknown; to a desert existence if you will. The week of January 17, 2022, Karl started complaining of his left leg and arm not being 'quite right'. He described it as a heavy feeling and maybe some tingling. He had an energy drink earlier in the week and thought maybe that just increased his blood pressure. While it was in the back of our minds, we didn't give it too much worry. On Thursday of that week, he went to the nurse as his place of employment. By this time, his foot was dragging a bit and he was not feeling well at all. His blood pressure was high. In fact, we later learned that the bottom number was over one hundred which is cause for concern of a stroke. He went to his primary care physician that Thursday. Unfortunately, after attempting to regulate his medicine, they sent him home. I could tell he was agitated and not feeling well. We both went to bed in hopes that all would be well in the morning. Little did we know a storm was coming. One that would change our lives forever and send us into a season of mourning.

The morning of January 21, 2022, Karl could not keep his balance. At one point I had to jump off the couch to keep him from falling into our glass front door. At that point I texted my daughter who is a nurse and works the night shift. I knew she was getting off work and would be able to respond to my text messages. I remember telling her all the details. Her text back was, "Mom, please get dad to the ER right away. It sounds like he is having a stroke." To this day, only six months later, I can't believe the presence of mind I had to remain calm and collected as we made the one-hour trek to the hospital.

While the stroke was confirmed on Friday, we were in good spirits despite it all. We were told that he would be out of the hospital by Sunday. That all changed Saturday morning when I arrived at the hospital. Karl could no longer move the left side of his body. There was feeling, but no movement. We were thrust into a season of mourning that would change the fabric of our lives.

As I sit here six months later, recounting the events of that week in January, I realize that there will probably always be a feeling of mourning around this life event. Perhaps the feeling is not as daunting as it once was, but when I stop and reflect on that week and the ten plus weeks of therapies, and 4-hour round trips to Kansas City, appointments too many to count, etc., I feel a sense of mourning well up in me. Now my response to it is different, however. I no longer stuff it down and put on a brave face or tell myself, "Well, at least, this or that." Instead, I acknowledge it. I am thankful for it because it means I am alive, and I feel deeply. I then choose to sit with it for as long as necessary. Mourning, she is a brilliant teacher.

Here is what mourning has taught me:

It is necessary. It sucks like hell, but it is necessary.

There is no timeline for your mourning. It may come and go in waves. It may last for more than a season or two—or three. You will have days filled with joy only to wake up one morning feeling as if you have been dragged backwards into sadness. May I just tell you it is all normal? My season(s) of mourning may or may not look like yours. Yours will not look like mine or anyone else's. Let me completely assure you that you are normal, whatever your season of mourning looks like.

Asking for help is bravery. After years of thinking I could get out of this season by myself, I finally sought professional counseling. I'm so glad I did this. While I still deal with aspects of my life, past and present, that cause me to mourn, I feel more empowered. I also have one person in my life (other than Karl) who I can call anytime, and we can literally talk about anything with no judgment. She can do the same with me. After years in church, I felt so isolated and wounded by people I thought I could trust. I shut down and didn't tell anyone any of my struggles. That includes Karl. For me this was incredibly unhealthy because my way of dealing with me was to stuff it all down and do my best to forget about my pain.

But when I started sharing, I also had to learn boundaries and take some amazing advice from Brene' Brown that not everyone has earned the right to hear your story. I and my story are incredibly sacred. You and your story are incredibly sacred, my friend! Not everyone will protect and give your story the respect and care it deserves. I did, however, find that one person who will sit with me in it—all of it—no matter how dark it gets! I am grateful for that.

# 19

# FINDING INHERITANCE IN THE DESERT

*"Blessed are the meek, for they shall inherit the earth."*

MATTHEW 5:5

## *Karl*

I once taught safety classes at my place of business. One class gets more "smirks" than the other classes, and I can understand why. It's called Active Shooter. It's where we prepare for the unlikely event of a mass shooter invading our company. We used the Department of Homeland Security model of "Run, Hide, Fight," which stresses that we try to run first, then hide, and if we have no other options, fight back. My coworkers' smirk because they probably own more guns per capita than any group on the planet—it's an obsession! In their minds, this is not how the *scenario plays out.* All of us have probably imagined a home invasion or an unlikely assault and how we would react in that situation. History shows that our imaginations are not close to reality, but we like to think we would be able to control the situation if it happened.

For the past 35 years (my adult life), I have become very proficient at being persistent. I always figured I could overcome my deficiencies by outworking, outthinking, or outlasting the competition (real or imagined). In my mind, I considered myself to be lacking in a few areas, but that would just cause people to underestimate me. I have been determined to surprise them with my tenacity (otherwise known as stubbornness). I achieved a lot of things, overcame some obstacles, and had some great adventures. However, in retrospect, I now feel that the best things I have accomplished are the things that were not obtained by my might or by my power or by my determination. The best things in my life have been the things that have come to me by my trust and submission—they were when I was meek.

The age-old question of "Who gets the earth?" probably started with Cain and Abel. As agriculture developed, the need for land increased and battles over what is "mine" (much like two toddlers) caused all kinds of disputes and struggles. Man's answer to this struggle was to get determined and take by force whatever they felt they had a right to. Since the Israelites believed they deserved the promised land, they took it by force. The Romans eventually gobbled up most of the known world only to be imitated by the British in a later era. To one degree or another, all these groups—and there have been many—have believed they had a right to what they were taking. When Americans arrived on this continent, we continued the pattern by annihilating the Indigenous and taking what we thought was "ours." But is this even close to what God intended? Could it be that somewhere along the way, we got it completely backward?

The Native Americans may have understood this better than anyone. The way that seems right to us is to capture what we feel we have a right to. It is not ours to capture—it is only God's to give.

And to whom does He give it? He gives it to the meek. This is the continuation of the forming of the new kingdom.

> "The renewal of the earth begins at Golgotha, where the meek one died, and from thence it will spread. When the Kingdom finally comes, the meek shall possess the earth." 28

Most societies assume that meekness is weakness, but maybe a more accurate description could be "power under control." Chromatus defines the meek as "those who are gentle, humble and unassuming, simple in faith and patient in the face of every affront."[29]

Jesus' ideal is certainly counterintuitive to the way we think. In the United States we almost value paranoia. We have intense anxiety over our security, especially national security. We feel a need to get to the top and "claw" our way there, feeling little remorse for the bodies we leave behind. Being the best is not just a hope—it's necessary. We feel we must be the best and almost any means justifies the end. Once we achieve success or acquire what we think we deserve, we believe we must do everything to protect what we have acquired. We then can justify all nature of things because we earned it and it's our right to defend it. My friends, none of this is what Jesus taught or modeled about how to inherit the earth.

## JESUS BLESSED THE MEEK (MATTHEW 5:5)

As the Roman soldiers (who had already conquered the world) looked on, Jesus told them that it's not them that will ultimately inherit the earth. They may have taken it, but it wasn't theirs to take. The people

---

**28** Bonhoeffer, Dietrich. *The Cost of Discipleship.* New York:Touchstone, 1995, 62–63

**29** https://www.christianitytoday.com/ct/2007/august/10.48.html

they probably never even acknowledged were those who would inherit the earth. Jesus continues his theme of a Kingdom that is not ruled by the powerful, or the determined, or even the ones with good five-year plans. This counter cultural ideal certainly must have piqued their curiosity, but probably got the same reaction as when I suggest that Jesus never taught to defend ourselves (at least not violently). I can imagine much of the crowd looking at each other trying to wrap their minds around this idea. "Who is this guy?"

### JESUS DESCRIBED HIMSELF AS MEEK (MATTHEW 11:29)

The reason Jesus can bring rest to our souls is because He is gentle (meek) and humble in heart. The weary and burdened can come to him and find an "easy yoke," not because he is controlling or needy, but because He is humble and unassuming. This is one of the most powerful statements about Jesus: The One that has all power and every right to demand and control and coerce chooses to be quiet and non-controlling. His power asserts itself in meekness. This is so powerful and challenging to me!

### JESUS DEMONSTRATED MEEKNESS (MATTHEW 21:5)

It is telling to look at the events of Passover at the end of Jesus' life. Pilate entered Jerusalem surrounded by soldiers, relying on the military strength of the empire. Jesus entered the city "humble" (meek), and "mounted on a donkey," surrounded by normal people. The soldiers were probably snickering again at this counter cultural display of meekness vs power. Years later, we now realize that the powerful empire of Rome is all but nonexistent and the Kingdom of Christ (inaugurated by a guy on a donkey) continues to spread across the globe. Jesus didn't use power to control, even though what He did was captivating. Jesus didn't use power to impress, even though what He did was impressive. In a way, He channeled His power into being meek.

Meekness is not a lack of power, but it is focusing the power we have in the right direction. Our typical behavior says to control our circumstances, situations, and outcomes. Jesus challenges us to control ourselves by channeling all that power He supplies into a gentleness that is *under* control, not *in* control. This gentle, unassuming power is what Jesus says inherits the earth.

Since we stopped going to church, many of our alliances and the things we relied on have been removed. Some of my income stream has been diminished because I'm not a pastor anymore. I thought about it when I published my first book. I thought, "Man, I could have sold a lot of books if I was still a Southern Baptist." Then I remembered that I would no longer want to author a book that most of them would read. There are advantages to alliances, but in a way, we experience God more directly when we are meek. Our inheritance is not through associations and organizations, it is through direct encounter. I'm experiencing this in the desert.

## *Laura*

Although my parent's marriage had its difficulties throughout their 25 years, they didn't divorce until I was 17. There were various times when they would separate for a time. It was then that I recognized just how strong of a role model my mom was. I am sure there is more history behind their divorce than I need to be aware of, but I get the feeling there were things in their marriage that catapulted my mom to become a strong, determined, take no bullshit from a man, type of woman. I admired her for that! I know because of her pain; she didn't want to see her girls go through the same types of things.

So, while I was quiet as a child, I learned that it was important to tell things like they were. I became so good at doing this that one day after I had laid it on the line to Karl, giving no thought to how my words would cut him, he said, "You get to say whatever you want. The problem is you don't see the bruised and bloody bodies you leave behind." I still remember that after all these years. That's how drastically it hit me. So, while my marriage was still a safe place to have my feelings heard, I had to learn to think before I spoke.

When Karl entered the ministry, I remember I really didn't have any feelings, positive or negative, about it. I just remember telling him, "I'm not going to be the typical pastor's wife." The message I got once we entered ministry was, "You will do whatever it takes to support your husband." In other words, be submissive; be meek. At that time, meekness meant weakness.

I did not get this message from Karl. However, when we would go to a convention that was supported by our denomination, that message became apparent. It wasn't overt; it was very subtle, but it was apparent. Women never spoke at these husband/wife gatherings. Their opinions were never sought after. They were, in my opinion, to be seen and not heard. I never considered myself "arm candy," but at these events, I kind of felt like I was more of a show piece than a valid participant in what I thought was "our" ministry.

Here is what the desert has taught me about being meek: Meekness is not about stripping a person of their identity. It is not about losing your voice. But it's also not about controlling and bullying people. Being meek is being who you are with gentleness and ease. It's being authentic. It means I can speak my truth and still show abundant grace while doing so, without being worried that I will leave bruised and bloody bodies in my wake. It is about power under control. Because of the Divine in me, I can have both. I understand that I can be powerful, but also self-controlled.

# 20

# FINDING SATISFACTION IN THE DESERT

*"Blessed are those who hunger and thirst for righteousness, for they will be filled."*

MATTHEW 5:6

## *Karl*

Songs often remind us that we still haven't found our final destination. Not only do we have a sense that we are not there yet, but often we are unsure of where we are going, or even what we hope to find once we get there.

The search for personal satisfaction and personal spirituality can get in the way of more comprehensive goals. I've often said, "I'm trying to figure out who I am," but just as often exclaimed, "I wish I knew what I was looking for!" One guy that was sure what he was pursuing was Martin Luther King Jr. He was one person who was sure about his purpose.

One of the things that King talked about a lot was justice. He once said, "True peace is not merely the absence of tensions, it is the presence of justice."[30] That is just brilliant! I don't even want to explain it because I'm afraid I would diminish it. He also said, "Injustice anywhere is a threat to justice everywhere."[31] Again, perfectly understandable, and hard to argue with—it's just true and easy to see what drove him to keep going. King also understood that things like justice take time to come to fruition. He stated, "The arc of the moral universe is long, but it bends toward justice."[32] At first glance, this doesn't seem to have anything to do with the 4th beatitude.

The Greek word, *dikaiosyne*, actually has a dual meaning: righteousness (which deals with our individual spirituality), and justice (which deals with setting things right in the world). God is not just interested in our spiritual condition, but also our social arrangements. Some literal interpretations of the word are "the state of man as he ought to be" and "the condition acceptable to God." Some early writers stressed that the word includes, "right conduct toward men and piety toward God." Maybe the clearest interpretation, and the inclination to use the word justice, is one interpretation: "the virtue which gives each one his due."

It is important that we recognize the importance of justice. My mother taught me to recognize the unfairness of the world. That is a good building block to equip us to face the world, understanding that life is unfair. But I am also blessed with a wife and three children that go beyond this acceptance of injustice. In a way, they can't accept it. Like Martin Luther King and Jesus, they are never satisfied with that

---

**30** https://quoteinvestigator.com/2020/11/26/true-peace/

**31** https://tssw.tulane.edu/news/injustice-anywhere-threat-justice-everywhere

**32** https://obamawhitehouse.archives.gov/blog/2011/10/21/arc-moral-universe-long-it-bends-toward-justice

injustice. They hunger and thirst—they long—for each person in the world to be given their due. They are amazingly fixed on the notion that justice is possible in this world. This kind of person just seems to want it a little more.

We also see this in the life and words of Jesus. He didn't criticize the poor—He reached down and lifted them up. He encouraged the more fortunate to look on others with compassion, not contempt. His concern certainly reached far beyond just that which affected Him personally. This beatitude stresses that thinking and working toward justice is not a fruitless endeavor. Righteousness and Justice are part of the same package. I don't pretend to understand that fully, but somehow, I know it's true.

I'm trying to allow myself to long for righteousness *and* justice. For me, that means longing for something that I can't produce on my own. It is hoping for something I often can't see any solutions to. Often, those are issues that seem unsolvable, like gun rights, immigration, racism, child hunger, and other social struggles. Jesus said he would satisfy that longing! Even though I don't understand how the thirst will be satisfied, I simply trust that it will! Like Martin Luther King Jr., I must stay hungry and not give up!

I remember various football coaches screaming at me to try harder, but it is the way they did it that was interesting. They would say "Do you want it?" Then they would scream, "How bad do you want it?" Then, they'd talk to each other, "I don't think he wants it. Doesn't look like he wants it!" It was kind of like a mild form of abuse, but it was usually effective. To most casual observers, it probably doesn't appear that we really care that much about justice for all. We give up too easily. Like my football coaches, I often wonder, "Do we want it?" Do we really want it? It doesn't look like we want it!"

When we care about the things that matter, we are satisfied in ways that are hard to explain and hard to quantify.

When I look at the life of Jesus, I notice that He suffered injustice personally. How fair is it that the most moral man ever suffered as much as anyone ever has? How just is it that He most often did not receive the respect He deserved or the treatment that was appropriate to His standing? He did exactly what the Father said, and yet usually was mistreated, misunderstood, and misrepresented. He certainly longed for justice and taught that justice was desirable and worthy of pursuit. It seems that through His personal journey of injustice, He was able to obtain justice for all of us (He set the world right). He was satisfied, in a way! King shows a similar pattern: he suffered and was killed, which helped bring justice to many.

Maybe that's a good lesson for us. Personal satisfaction and personal justice may need to be sacrificed or delayed for the pursuit of justice for a larger group. Maybe, that is the satisfaction this beatitude is talking about. Maybe it's something for the future. Like the song writers, I still haven't found it, but I'm willing to keep looking for real satisfaction and real justice. I didn't always find it in organized religion, but I'm seeing a glimpse of it here in the desert.

## *Laura*

I understand life is not fair, but it has always been my mission to make things as fair as possible. I come by it quite honestly. When my sisters and I started having our babies, my mom would always be sure that all the grandbabies had an equal number of gifts each Christmas. If she were out and found another gift for one grandchild, she would have to make sure that she got just one more thing for all the others because it had to be fair. I found myself doing the same thing as my children grew up, and now my grandchildren are the benefactors of this "it has to be fair" mentality. While this mindset might be hard on the budget, it is something that I think has been ingrained in me. Things may not always be fair, but if it's up to me, I'm going to make it as close to fair as I can.

I think this mentality has always been a part of who I am. When I was forty, I got a wild hair and decided to go back to school to get my Masters in Elementary Education. I say "wild hair" because I was the mom who would do anything for my kids' teachers, but I would always tell them that I'm grateful they are teachers because I could never do what they do—famous last words. If I have ever had a calling in my life, it was when I was forty and seriously felt called to teach. It is one of the hardest things I've ever done. Managing a class full of energetic 6-, 7-, and 8-year-olds will age you fast. I'm confident I am keeping Miss Clairol in business. However, I would not change a thing about what I do.

Through teaching, I have learned to love such a variety of children. I am learning that each of them needs an advocate; someone who doesn't care what their last name is or how much money their parents make. They need someone to believe in them despite all of that. Someone who will be their voice when others want to silence them as a lost cause. Sometimes in small rural towns, what matters most is your name. It determines many times how people during your school career will think and look upon you. I was never from these towns, so names didn't matter to me. They could be the principal's child, or they could be the child with parents that have been in trouble with the law since they were in school. It didn't matter to me. They were one of my students, regardless. No matter where they fell on the economic, behavioral, or academic continuum, when they entered my classroom, they were loved, and the expectations were the same for everyone.

Being a grandmother has only reinforced this idea of fairness in me. I have three amazing grandchildren, Hollyn, Jackson, and Sloane. My heart exploded wide open when Hollyn was born. Everything leading up to, and including, her birth is what would be considered "typical." She was my first grandchild, so everything that her mom would share with me, I was amazed and delighted about! When she was born, my heart's capacity to love burst wide open. She has met her developmental milestones and with each one, we rejoiced! She learned her ABC's and all her letter sounds at the age of two! As a teacher, I couldn't be prouder of her, and I can't wait for the day she reads to me!

About a year and a half later we found out we were going to be grandparents again! I remember the day exactly! It was Valentine's Day, 2017 and we were in a local McAllister's restaurant having lunch with both daughters and their husbands. Lily handed me a red box as a Valentine's gift. I thought this was a bit strange since we didn't typically exchange gifts on Valentine's Day. I opened it and inside was a tiny, crocheted baby's hat. I screamed! I was so excited that I would once again have someone calling me "Mimi!" Jackson's development in utero and birth were not "typical." As I mentioned earlier, at 20 weeks gestation, Lily and Trevor found out that Jackson had contracted a congenital virus called Cytomegalovirus or CMV. Typically, CMV doesn't cause any issues in people outside of utero, but in utero, it carries many complications. It can cause premature birth, small head/brain size, cerebral palsy, as well as additional developmental issues. Jackson has experienced most of these issues, including being born two months premature.

While I held Hollyn hours after she was born, I wasn't able to hold Jackson for at least 6 weeks after he was born. Jackson is doing well in a unique way. He is thriving! He is happy and healthy! He laughs and smiles and has the cutest pair of glasses I have ever seen! He is now almost 18 months old. There are many things he can't do that a typical 18-month-old can, but there are so many things he does that bring me an abundant amount of delight.

I like to think as a teacher, and especially as a Mimi, I am walking in the ways of Jesus. He did not show partiality to anyone; instead, He loved all despite their name and position, or their emotional, mental, or spiritual health. It didn't matter, and it shouldn't matter to us. There are people all around us on the fringes that are looking for someone to say, "I see you. I hear you. You have value and worth, not because of who you are or what you've done, but just because you exist."

My experience has been that all people are not created equal in the typical church. Only one person gets to speak on Sunday morning. Only a few people get to lead from the stage and most church buildings are not very handicapped accessible. It's typical to exclude people that are difficult or too different. It's just easier to keep order in any organization when someone is in control, and we know what to expect daily from the people in leadership. Believe it or not, Karl and I have observed a noticeable inner circle at several churches we have been involved with. When we talk about it, we understand it, but it's much harder to be "fair" when the game starts with inequalities. In the desert, we are finding a more level playing field like we heard about in the New Testament.

I'm finding that justice and fairness is not so much about making sure everyone gets the same gifts. Maybe, it's more about my attitude. It's about how I treat people just like I do my students. Maybe it is true what Jesus said: Those that hunger and thirst for justice will be satisfied.

All I can do is have the right attitude and treat people fairly—And that's enough.

21

# FINDING MERCY IN THE DESERT

*"Blessed are the merciful, for they shall receive mercy."*

MATTHEW 5:7

## *Karl*

I have had a lot of time to think over the past few years. Because of my deconstruction, I separated from many of my friends, and later stopped going to church altogether. By taking some time to self-evaluate, I found areas of my life where I was often judgmental and retributive. I used to think that some people are just worse than others and they deserve what they get.

When I was young, I often heard the expression, "You made your bed, now you have to lie in it." People used this message because they didn't want to have to deal with tricky situations. In a way, it was a twisted sense of justice. Most of us could easily see ourselves in similar situations as those that made mistakes, but we wanted to make sure they suffered a little, so they wouldn't make that mistake again. Sometimes, it makes us feel justified if they are punished. Even though we feel some sympathy for them, we figure they "got what they deserved."

The problem is that this is not the attitude of Jesus. Sometimes our circumstances are what we need to teach us (discipline us). But ultimately what we really need is mercy, not because God is punishing us, but because life is hard.

The Pharisees were usually people that showed little mercy. Jesus talked about one of them that prayed in the middle of the street. He said, "I am thankful that I am not like other people…like this tax collector," (Luke 18). Then, he proceeded to tell God what he had accomplished. There it is: the need to feel superior! It derails the plan for mercy. The tax collector could have responded with his list of accomplishments, but he chose to respond with the only proper response to life's woes, "God, be merciful to me, the sinner." It's a choice—the loud and proud proclamation of our worth, and our judgment of others, or the honest plea for mercy. Jesus said that the prayer for mercy connected (justified) him because he was humble. Again, it is not because God is punishing us, but sometimes others are.

Justice often implies that something is due to us. Instead of demanding favor for ourselves, maybe we could hope for relief for underserved people. These might be people that work hard, and try, and still cannot get what should be due to them. We could fight for them and try to help lift them up from the imbalance of life. Some people don't have bootstraps to pull up. Sometimes, our actions can only be classified as a gift (grace). Very often, I do something for my children that they don't deserve, or that they didn't ask for. If I send them money electronically, I sometimes put in the memo section, "just because." But mercy is not just for the under-served—it is for the undeserving. Mercy is for the sinner—and sinners are us! Mercy is very literally *not getting what we deserve.*

It is hard to receive mercy if we don't have an attitude of mercy for others. When we give people just what we think they deserve, it's hard to imagine God or others would show us mercy.

It's interesting how connected the beatitudes are. It's hard to imagine a heart of mercy without being *poor in spirit,* which is the first beatitude. When we are too spiritual and don't realize our own poverty, we punish others instead of showing mercy. It's also hard to imagine a heart of mercy without the second beatitude, a heart that *mourns.* When we see ourselves and others as we really are, we know that we need mercy and others need it from us. It's hard to imagine a heart of mercy without the third beatitude, *meekness.* Whatever power we possess to destroy our enemies must be brought *under control* in order to show mercy. It's hard to imagine a heart of mercy without the fourth beatitude, *longing for righteousness and justice.* Sometimes others need to be lifted up; sometimes they need something they don't deserve; but, more often, it's better to not give them what they deserve—that is mercy!

Imagine someone at work yells at you. For some of us, that doesn't take a creative imagination. Afterward, the two of you don't speak to each other for a couple of days. You know you need to forgive them. While you agree that they deserve to be told off or put in their place, the path to forgiveness needs mercy, not judgment. The offense is obvious and easy to critique, but the solution is harder.

The story of Joseph shows us a rather good example of mercy. After his brothers sell him into slavery, he recovers from the trauma and eventually oversees everything his brothers need and want during the famine. What a wonderful opportunity to get them back! When they said, "we are your slaves," he could have had the biggest get-even party ever—they were at his disposal. Talk about justice! Most of us might have even encouraged him to make them pay! They made their bed, now they were going to have to lie in it. Instead, Joseph says, "Am I in the place of God?" and he shows them mercy. He may have wrongly assumed God is retributive, but at least he understood how *godly* it is to be merciful.

I assume we are afraid that people won't be reformed unless we punish them for their actions. Jesus said, "I desire mercy, not sacrifice." He taught us that it is not when we find atonement but when we find forgiveness. And forgiveness comes through mercy. If mercy is not expressed, we tend toward perpetual punishment. Maybe that's where we imagined some of our ideas about what hell really is. If we forgo mercy, we keep others and ourselves in slavery to the incident or the behavior. The unresolved battle lingers and festers usually into something worse.

Jesus didn't just preach that the beatitudes were right, he lived them. Mercy is no exception. His life showed that he believed in showing mercy. He didn't give people what they deserved; His disciples should probably be thankful for that. Jesus as a revelation of God did not act in retribution—he showed mercy!

I am thankful that God often lifts us up when we are *underserved.*

I am thankful that He also gives us grace that is *undeserved.*

## *Laura*

I shared in an earlier chapter that one of my greatest character traits is compassion. As I write this chapter, I need to come clean. Mercy and compassion are quite easy for me to extend when it is given to those living in the margins. It is easy to grant it to people who are hurting. In other words, compassion comes easy when I am showing it to those who are not in any way hurting me. However, there is definitely the side of me who, when hurt, wants to see that person hurt as well, not physically, but emotionally. In other words, I want them to feel the same way they made me feel. This is definitely not the most attractive side of my personality. I would much rather only tell you about the side of me that shows abundant mercy. The truth is, we have all had our capacity to show mercy challenged by others.

Being wounded is something many of us are familiar with, inside and outside of the institution of church. My first bona fide experience with genuine wounding started about 25 years ago. I am not even sure how to start this because when I think about it, it still doesn't make any sense to me. About a half a decade ago, my father stopped all communication with my sisters and me. I've reached out to him, but never heard back. This led me into a downward spiral, wondering what I had done to cause him to *disown* me. The more I tried over the years to come to some conclusion as to why, it only added to my hurt and anger. How could he live with himself knowing he has several grandchildren and great grandchildren he would never meet? To this day, I still have no answers.

Oddly, this type of thing showed up in all of the churches Karl pastored. We would go into these churches that were on the verge of closing their doors. They would treat Karl as if he were there to bring this church back from the brink of death. People were so welcoming. Women flocked around me, wanted to know me, and loved our children. It all seemed to be going really well. Not living around family, it really felt like we were all family. Something would happen and, what was once like a loving family relationship, went south really fast. I can't speak for Karl, but the way it played out for me is women just stopped talking to me, much like my dad. I had no idea why. I even went up to some of the women and asked if I had done anything to offend them. They would look at me like I had the plague, tell me "No," and go on ignoring me.

The connection I began to make is that this is how family treats family. My dad. The church. It made me incredibly sad and led to so much self-doubt. I was the "common denominator" in all of these situations, so it must be me.

Mercy is the ability to show forgiveness or compassion to someone when you would rather hurt them. I've heard it said a hundred times, "Hurt people, hurt people," and while I am not at all spiritually bypassing my pain or anyone else's who might be reading this chapter, there is truth behind this quip. I can say that because when I was hurt by these people, including my dad, I wanted them to hurt, too. That is a natural, human response. But thinking this way ultimately led me to the realization that the person I had the least amount of mercy for was me. Living with the anger, hurt, and resentment left me in a place where I didn't like myself at all.

My process of healing was not an easy one and it is still ongoing. As I stated before, Karl and I went through an immersive experience called BreakThrough with HeartConnexion Ministries. In fact, we went through it twice! That is not a sad thing! I'm so grateful we had the opportunity to do that. I have also talked to several spiritual directors and read countless books, my favorites being all those written by Brené Brown. One of the main things I learned from all of her books is to set boundaries. I learned that this was a big issue for me. As long as I can remember, I have never wanted to disappoint others, which means my boundaries were very weak. For me, setting boundaries was a way of showing myself mercy. It was a way of showing myself the love and compassion I had failed to show to others and myself.

One of the most controversial things I had to do in order to show mercy was to leave church. I had to leave the place where I was not only being wounded, but wounding others, because I was not emotionally and spiritually available to give to others in that space. Since leaving, I have gained peace. This is how I know it is the right decision for me at this moment. I will not say this is permanent, and I will not say that it is not. This is where I am today, and it is good.

Walking in this desert is where I am able to find mercy for myself and for others. I am able to sit with myself, speak kindly to myself, and forgive myself. The same can be true for those who have hurt me. For my dad: I still don't understand. It still hurts. But I do not live in that hurt anymore. I wish him so much goodness in the rest of the life he has left. I want him to find happiness and peace and forgiveness for himself and others. I really do! I hope the very same for those in the churches we pastored. I no longer wish them the same hurt, or any hurt. I hope they can find truth in how they have treated us and others, but even if they don't, I no longer have to be bound to them with my anger. And to the church: I hope she can find her way back to the unfailing love of Jesus—for all people. I hope one day she is truly that place of healing, a place of refuge, and a place of abundant mercy.

Until then, I am the sanctuary, and in me I will strive to show these things to me. In doing so, I can show them to the world.

# 22

# FINDING VISION IN THE DESERT

*"Blessed are the pure in heart, for they shall see God."*

MATTHEW 5:8

## *Karl*

Vision has always been an issue for me. For as long as I can remember, I have had strong glasses and issues with my physical sight. My parents first had me evaluated when I was sitting inches away from the television. I remember wearing prisms on my glasses because I had a "lazy" eye, but just the magnification required in my prescription is obvious and has been since I was young. I suppose it's just part of my identity. My nickname was "blind man" in high school. I don't remember resenting it necessarily, although I did get contacts as soon as I possibly could.

The Bible has a lot to say about vision. One common theme is the idea that we can have eyes but not really see. Man, I can relate to that! I couldn't tell you scientifically why my physical eyes don't work so well without correction. According to Jesus, the eyes that see God are connected to the purity of our heart. It's as simple as that!

Jesus also said that a hardened heart contributes to this condition of having eyes that don't see (Mark 8:17). I've always been sure that I didn't want to have a hardened heart, but what are the things that lead us there? What hardens our hearts? What keeps us from seeing?

My heart is often hardened by *selfishness*. "What's in it for me?" "When do I get my chance?" "I deserve whatever I decide is best for this particular moment." Selfishness centers on what I deserve and what I have a right to. It leads me away from the great commandment and the Golden Rule. It devastates intimacy with God and replaces it with a kind of self-appeasement—I wouldn't even call it nurturing because, in the end, it's not that good for me.

My heart is also hardened by *judgmentalism*. Someday, I hope this isn't on my list, but today, and yesterday, and the day before, I struggled with this unholy, unnecessary, unfruitful practice that does nothing but harden my heart, destroy my influence, and cloud my ability to see God in every situation. Maybe it's where I start. In my mind, I want to notice those things that are askew and bring attention to them. But, like Paul, I need to pray that I will see with the eyes of my heart (Ephesians 1:18) instead of just my ocular senses and my judgmental reasoning.

My heart is also hardened by *busyness*. I'm challenged to live a more quiet and contemplative life, but I'm also excited by a life of activity. This is certainly a balance between productivity, accomplishment, sincerity, purpose, and soul care—and a dozen other things. I'm challenged to imagine a life led by what my heart knows is right instead of what excited me most recently. I think this would be something like seeing more clearly.

When David said, "Create in me a clean heart," he was using the same language as Jesus. David sensed that he couldn't change his behavior until he changed what he saw, and somehow was able to understand that seeing begins with the heart. He needed to be pure in heart to see God. I long for this unclouded vision in my heart much like I long to have 20/20 vision in my eyes.

You see when our hearts are pure, we see God not just eventually, but presently. When our hearts are pure, we see God first in ourselves. Recognizing God's leading and teaching and correction in our lives becomes a reality, not just a hope. Stripped of our self-interest, we see how God wants to interact with us much like the Father, Son, and Spirit exist in perfect harmony. A pure heart guides us to better awareness and stronger vision of God's activity in and around us.

Seeing God in ourselves is important. Seeing God in others is life changing. A pure heart helps us consider the needs, motivation, and struggles of others before we rush to make judgments and pronounce verdicts. In fact, when our hearts are pure, we can give up the need to change people and understand that God can and will change their lives. Oh, that we could be pure in heart enough to see through the eyes of Jesus: eyes of compassion; eyes of love; eyes of grace!

When we are pure in heart, we also see the rest of the world—we see God in creation. The pure in heart see that God is interested in the care and comfort of everything in nature. They are not just to be used—they are to be cared for. A pure heart can see this! It sees God in creation.

For years, pastors have admonished us to change what we look at. There is obviously some truth to this. But, most likely, what is important is to change *how* we see what we look at. We can't change those things by judging or condemning them, and we can't always avoid them. We need a new vision to see things differently! We need vision that can see God in every circumstance! New vision, which sees God, comes from a pure heart!

For Laura and me, it was important to get outside the walls of organized religion to get a clearer vision of God. There were too many things blocking my view of the restorative, Christlike God that I was coming to know. There were too many things that were idols and not helpful to my journey. My heart wasn't pure, and there were too many things vying for my attention and shielding my view. Just like mindfulness is helping me to think clearly, the openness of the desert is helping my heart become pure, and my eyes to see what truly Divine is.

## *Laura*

For me, the scariest thing about entering the desert was that I had no immediate direction or vision. I didn't know where to go or what to do. There were no obvious paths and no signs to mark the way. The pain of our ministry was in some strange way preparing me for the desert, and it seemed like overnight that it became my new permanent residence. It wasn't where I chose to be, but it seemed like where I needed to be. Everything was strange and dark. Nothing felt comforting or familiar. I suddenly felt empty, deserted in the desert. Not even God was there at that moment.

I was sure in an instant I became an atheist. It wasn't even a conscious decision that I made to become one! As I mentioned earlier, the moment I held our first granddaughter to my heart, everything I knew I had experienced inside my religion and my church was wrong. The vision of the God of my past was one of retribution. He was distant. He was performance based. He was a "he." He was just like my earthly father; He wasn't around and wouldn't talk to me, and it was somehow my responsibility that He was this way.

This was my picture and my personal experience with God prior to the desert; prior to holding Hollyn to my heart only moments after she was born. So, I guess you could say that I entered the desert the same day Hollyn was born. It was most definitely not where I chose to be, but it was where I needed to be. It was only by accepting my place in this barren destination that I would finally be able to begin to get a new vision of the Divine.

For me, I could not get a sharp vision of the Divine without wrestling with everything I once knew. The questions started coming, and I am grateful that they are still a part of who I am today. I had to allow myself to sit alone, to have grace for myself, to forgive myself, and to trust myself in the desert space. The desert is vast and wide. It takes time to reach the next destination. I had to be patient with myself in the journey. I have had to conclude that having all the answers is not the answer, but if I can keep my eyes open, and wonder, and seek, my vision can become clearer.

Looking back, I would say the day I entered the desert was more of a spiritual breakthrough than a spiritual breakdown. I picture a wrecking ball breaking through the walls of a dilapidated building. Inside that building everything is dark and cold; it is musty with cobwebs everywhere. It is cloudy and dirty and uninhabitable. When the wrecking ball crashes through, it allows light to penetrate the dark spaces. It opens the once confined, stagnant space up to a fresh new breath of air. Once the dust has settled from the wreckage, our vision can become clearer. All the questions do not disappear, but there is more room for them. The doubts are not gone, but they are welcomed. There is more room. My vision of the Divine now has room to grow. The vastness of the desert allows her to expand and grow and thrive.

23

# FINDING PEACE IN THE DESERT

*"Blessed are the peacemakers, for they should be called sons of God."*

MATTHEW 5:9

## *Karl*

I have seen some pretty amazing fights break out during the time shortly after the death of a loved one. Many times, it involves who gets the stuff left behind. It's too bad, really! I don't know whether there will be much inheritance from my mother if she ever passes away. At this point, I sometimes wonder whether she will outlive me. If she does pass before me, I will have to split the inheritance with three brothers and a sister, so it's hard to imagine that any inheritance would be large enough to change my lifestyle. I don't think about it too much. All this is assuming she doesn't disown me at some time in the future!

Jesus left an inheritance to us through the disciples and the Holy Spirit. He said, "My peace, I give to you." If we were using our standard to measure peace (absence of strife), we probably would assume the disciples missed it somehow. Maybe they weren't there at the reading of the will. Most of them, if not all, were persecuted and martyred for following Jesus. Do we need to look again at the translation? Maybe Jesus meant something different.

We know Jesus was interested in peace by the number of times He talked about it. Also, He is described as the "Prince of Peace."

Maybe Martin Luther King Jr., a peace advocate, can help us out. He once said,

> "True peace is not the absence of tension; it is the presence of justice."[33]

I have always said peace is the presence of God. Peace can be found in the most unpeaceful situations. Throughout history, man has tried to build walls to create peace. We assume if we could block out all the ugly or evil or noise, then we would have peace. History teaches us that often it is the wall that is bringing hostility. Paul said that Christ brings down the "dividing wall of hostility." The most visible example in our time would be when Ronald Reagan stood at the Brandenburg Gate and said, "The advance of human liberty can only strengthen the cause of peace."[34] He later made the famous exclamation, "Mr. Gorbachev, tear down this wall."[35]

When we stopped going to church, or when we stepped away from the organizational church, it would be easy to assume that everything became peaceful. Certainly, there was more "quiet," but that doesn't necessarily mean that we were automatically overcome with peace.

---

**33** https://quoteinvestigator.com/2020/11/26/true-peace/

**34** https://www.reaganlibrary.gov/archives/speech/remarks-east-west-relations-brandenburg-gate-west-berlin

**35** https://www.reaganlibrary.gov/archives/speech/remarks-east-west-relations-brandenburg-gate-west-berlin

Peace is somewhat of a natural thing, but it isn't automatic. We can become peacemakers when we get deliberate about it. My motto these days is "I am learning to be at peace." When I think about "making" peace, I think about the following things.

## WE MUST MAKE PEACE WITH OUR PAST

Yesterday is a check that we already cashed. A friend recently reminded me that we did the best we could with the resources we had in the past. No matter how much we regret our past choices, we can't change what happened in the past. However, we can negatively affect the present by lingering in the past.

I often talk about the shadow work I did recently. Our shadow is the part of us where we have stuffed the painful experiences of our past. If we have not effectively addressed these issues, we will have issues like reactivity and anger in the present. Those situations are very much not like peace, they are more like the opposite. But my spiritual directors have taught me that we don't eradicate the shadow, we have to encounter it. Some call this "making friends with our shadow" while others just say, "we must be able to look upon our inner child with compassion." When I did this necessary work, guess what? I found, and am finding, more peace in my life. It is a one-to-one correlation—one of the best things I have ever done.

## WE MUST MAKE PEACE WITH OURSELVES

*"If you cannot find peace within yourself, you will never find it anywhere else."* [36]

---

**36** https://www.brainyquote.com/quotes/marvin_gaye_361092

We spend a good portion of our lives trying to create situations. We long to manipulate our environment enough to give us the results we desire. Often, what we control doesn't make our world any safer, but only brings us more anxiety. Not to mention, we slowly cease to live life while trying to control it. I suspect peace is something of a decision. If we want, we can choose to be happy. Call it joy or whatever sounds more holy, but peace is a choice. We can be content, and we can be at peace if we really want to. Remember the beatitude that said we could be satisfied if we just got a little hungrier for justice? Maybe King was right.

## WE MUST MAKE PEACE WITH OUR ENEMIES

*"People are hard to hate close up. Move in."*[37]

Violence, hatred, and bitterness have never achieved peace. They make us feel good for an instant but it's just an artificial high that won't last. Being retributive may get results, but it never achieves anything noble. People we make peace with may or may not change, but that is their decision. I have to do what I can to make peace with them. A friend reminded me that reconciliation is not always possible, but that doesn't mean I can't find peace with my enemies.

Peace is a decision, and it is a Jesus-type idea. We are highly creative at separating Jesus from His ideas. We like to recreate Him in our own image. Just like Jesus was very consistent in His message of non-violence, He was also consistent with the peace message.

---

**37** Brown, Brene, *Braving the Wilderness: The Quest for True Belonging and the Courage to Stand Alone*. New York: Random House, 2017, 63

As children of God, it is important that we accept the inheritance of peace that Jesus left us. Once accepted, we can make peace with our past, make peace with ourselves, and make peace with others.

It truly is a decision.

## *Laura*

I am a self-confessed future tripper. A future tripper is someone who worries about things that may or may not happen in the future. This practice promotes a great deal of anxiety in my body. I am waiting many times for the other shoe to drop, so to speak. As I'm writing this, I just heard the news that famed basketball player, Kobe Bryant and his daughter were killed in a helicopter crash.

At times like this, most of us think, *tell people you love them; hug your babies tighter—you never know how long you have.* While people can say such things and move on with life, I take it a step, sometimes several steps, further. I start thinking how he probably never realized that at the beginning of this year he would no longer be with us. That leads to me thinking that maybe I won't make it through this year or the next. This leads to envisioning my children crying at my funeral and not being able to watch my grandbabies grow up.

As you might guess, there is truly little peace in this way of thinking. I'm not sure where it originates, but I'm grateful to be aware of it so I can speak kindly when I am experiencing it. I can investigate practices that might help me breathe through these times. I am learning that speaking kind words during unrest can be extremely healing.

We don't have to look far to see unrest. It's all around us, not just across the world, but even in our own neighborhoods. There are the big issues like war and famine, but also concerns with the homeless or the hungry. There is unrest when there are unkind words being said between coworkers or when someone cuts me off in traffic. There is unrest in our churches where wounded people sit. They wait patiently to be healed from the pain, only to be further injured by the very institution that promised them relief. But unrest doesn't just fall on us from somewhere, it originates in the hearts of real people.

For me, my states of unrest come from a desire to control the various situations I am a part of and then realizing that I cannot. Mind you, there are some parts of it I can control, but there are parts I can't. While I can control my driving, I cannot control that of others. I can control the words that come out of my mouth about my coworkers, but I cannot control what others might do or say. I can in turn control my response to their words, but I can't control how they respond to me. I can help at a soup kitchen or walk a 5K to raise money for the homeless, but I can't always change their situation like I want. When I focus on the abundance of issues, problems, and "what if's," I often become completely overwhelmed.

However, lately, I have been finding peace in a most unlikely place. The desert. I know that it seems like an unlikely place. In the past, when I would think of the desert, I would have hardly thought of it as a place of "peace." The desert is a dry land that has little water. It is barren. It is expansive and it must be lonely. Despite all of that, I am finding peace here.

The desert has a great deal of solitude; a place where I am alone with myself for an extended period of time. I didn't always find this comforting. I am learning that to draw nourishment from the desert, I have to be extremely authentic, and I have to have grace for myself. To find peace here, I have to be exactly where I am today. In the desert, many days, the only voice I hear is my own, and that of the Divine. As we walk together in this desert, the Divine's words are comforting and loving. Anything other than that is my own voice. I am learning to listen more to Her voice because She speaks the truth.

For me personally to find peace in the desert, I had to leave organized religion. This move thrust us out into the desert and into this desert sanctuary. I didn't see this separation from the church as a "peaceful" move. In fact, initially we lost our entire perceived community. Today, I only have one faithful friend left from all of our former community. Everyone else has faded away.

Not only was the desert hot, dry, and vast, but it can also be eerily silent and lonely. In retrospect, this was necessary for me. There is no peace in a place where you try to be something you are not; while people are telling you that you are not doing enough to measure up. It is exhausting living in a fishbowl, or mindlessly going around the hamster wheel. There is no peace. Since leaving church, I am alone—just me and the Divine. Most days we just commune together. We are just together. No expectations or hoops to jump through.

I wish I could tell you that I no longer future trip. I just did it today! I'm not looking to be miraculously healed here in the desert. Instead, I am learning to live with myself as a beloved of the Divine. There will always be days when the Divine must entertain all my various questions and doubts and concerns. I don't think they mind. They let me cry and feel what I am feeling.

But regardless of the struggle, I now find peace even in the midst of the unrest. I still question and wrestle and struggle, and in the middle of it all, I realize I am loved and accepted exactly where I am. To me, that is peace. Many people have said it in various ways. Peace is not the cessation of anything, but it is about love and acceptance during the struggle. I'm glad I am finding it here in the desert.

## 24

# A FINAL WORD TO DESERT DWELLERS

We didn't author this book to tell anyone else what to do. By the time it is published, I may not even agree with it, because we are on a journey of discovery. Like my other four books, we simply wanted to keep a journal of our excursion in hopes that it might help someone else in their personal pilgrimage out into the desert. The desert really is beautiful. Like others who have walked here before, we hope you take the journey that you need to take. Life passes too quickly to walk in the steps that are ordained by someone else.

When I was a kid, I used to burn ants with a magnifying glass. Later, as a teenager, I would shoot sparrows out of the tree next to the church with my friend Jeff and his pellet gun. It was fun to me, and it seemed like a reasonable thing to do at the time. At some point, I developed a little more compassion for animals and other creatures, but initially, it seemed like my right as a superior being to do what I wanted with the inferiors.

It is important in life to grow in our understanding of things. It's hard to imagine that I knew everything about life, the world, and especially my faith at age seven, or even at twenty-one, or thirty-one. Over the years, I have questioned my understanding of life, politics, ethics, and even my spiritual beliefs. In all areas, I have found this process not to be dangerous, but helpful. I always grow, and grow up, when I ask good questions.

In many cases, even the early writers of the Bible were limited in their understanding. Assuming they had a pure understanding of the revelation of God would seem to be at least, a little misguided. This picture would not be completely painted until Jesus finished His mission and inaugurated the New Kingdom. And two thousand years later, I contest that we still don't completely understand what Jesus was trying to say!

Several years ago, I began to ask questions again. It led to some necessary and beneficial growth. I started by stating, "I have a suspicion that I may be wrong about some things." As I said, this may sound risky to most people, but I found it to be necessary for my growth. We cannot just rely on what we inherited. Sometimes we must go back further. Sometimes, we have to ask more questions.

# AFTERWORD

It has been a couple of years since we wrote the original manuscript for this book. In that short amount of time, things have changed. As we mentioned in the beginning, some of our views have evolved over time. We anticipated this would happen—and it did!

One of the reasons organized religion fails is that it wants to write its dogma and beliefs in stone. We all know from experience that as we grow and as things change, sometimes our beliefs and practices must change as well.

To make a long story short, our concerns about organized religion have only increased. We both feel that we may never go back to attending religious services, especially in American, Evangelical institutions. The feelings we have in this area have only become stronger over the past two years.

One of the new arguments we have, here in the desert, is people contending that we need to save the *faith*. They talk about preserving that faith for their grandchildren. But when we discuss this further, a subtle inconsistency emerges.

We find that what they are really talking about is preserving their religion. We can maintain our faith on an island with no other people. We can hold fast to our beliefs even if we're the last person on earth.

Many of these people have deconstructed their faith from a conservative, evangelical one to a more Christ-centered, usually more progressive mindset. Then, many of them joined a mainline denomination or transformed their church with great pain to be more orthodox and/or more "woke".

We applaud them for making these changes, especially when it causes them to be more open and affirming to the queer community and more empowering to women. But because they are still doubling down on their religion, what they are protecting is their practices.

We haven't quite realized that all religious practices are man-made. At some point we invented them, because we thought they would be effective to help us do whatever we thought we should do for God and ourselves. But when these practices have systemic problems because they are part of an organization, we need to solve the inherent problems or we will continue to make the same mistakes, even though our rituals are slightly better.

One of the ways people defend this position is to imply that some people deconstructed too much until nothing was left.

## CAN WE DECONSTRUCT TOO MUCH?

This is a common fear associated with deconstructing. People wonder whether they will have anything left if they keep asking questions and keep taking down the walls and structures that they have built up over time in their belief system.

In general, people interchange words like faith, Christianity, and beliefs and end up confusing themselves as to exactly what they are evaluating or removing. In this discussion, we wanted to clarify some of those words and how they relate to deconstruction. But first, understand this:

> "You can't destroy or deconstruct something that is eternal. If it is real, and/or truth, it can only grow stronger with your honest consideration. To me, it is like a refining. It gets purer."

**Christ:** For the sake of argument, let's consider Christ as eternal and something that can't be diminished. Our faith or allegiance or respect for the eternal Christ should grow stronger with questioning and consideration. As some are prone to imply, maybe we need to take the varnish off the image we had and "restore" a truthful understanding

**Religion/Christianity:** This is the part that man created and developed over time. Our practices are not sacred, we are simply addicted to them. This is not the part of the equation we need to be doggedly dedicated to.

**Faith:** This is confused with religion. My beliefs will change over time, and certainly in deconstruction. I'm allowed to believe what I want and refine those beliefs when I discover the truth; but when I turn it into a creed and make it static, then it just morphs into a religion/system to control others. The opposite of faith is certainty.

**Church:** the organizational structures we have developed over time are mostly not relevant for the 21st century. The internet has rendered them all but obsolete. Most are plagued with toxicity and produce trauma. They are breeding grounds for political unrest and there are better ways to heal, thrive and grow and we don't need professional clergy. If, by church, you mean loving your neighbor, then, "yes."

Otherwise, why don't we just evolve as people and if we discover we still need religion, we can resurrect it properly.

In my experience, the people that go all the way with deconstruction, usually end up with something purer and more lasting. The things that are real survive, the things that were manufactured and superficial, fall away. They find healing and peace and no longer need institutions or belief systems or superficial creedal alliances to the past. They are living present and authentic lives because they have gone inward instead of looking upward and been able to throw off the baggage involved with man-made systems.

## COVID-19

When we initially wrote this manuscript, the COVID-19 pandemic was just beginning. We were in the initial stages of experimenting with not attending religious services. This became almost mandatory for most people when the crisis became more serious. People were actually forced, sometimes by local ordinance, to not attend church.

The more responsible churches were more careful and stopped meeting for longer periods of time, and other pastors and congregations defied advice and braved the pandemic, sometimes with negative consequences.

So, what happened after people stayed away from church for a while? Did they realize they didn't need it as much as they thought they needed it? Or did it make them long for community and then they grew stronger?

Some of these questions are hard to answer, because the church was already in decline in America, and by 2018, the group known as *Nones* (the unaffiliated), became larger than Evangelicals.

A recent study[38] evaluated church attendance decline after COVID-19. Results showed that church attendance is down somewhere between 6 and 7% from 2019. Underlying reasons and causes of this are probably varied, but my assumption is that people realized in the 21st century that they don't need it as much as they thought they did.

Of course, these results are not in any way conclusive, but it is in some ways a confirmation of our suspicions.

---

**38** https://ifstudies.org/blog/the-decline-in-church-attendance-in-covid-america

## THE DEPTHS OF OUR DECLINE

On January 6th, 2021, Donald J. Trump, our former president, incited a riot that led to an insurrection of our government for the first time in history. He was trying to force his own vice president, Mike Pence, to subvert the will of the people and alter the results of the election.

If successful, one man (the vice president), would have been able to essentially decide who gets elected president of the United States. He refused to do so and the mob, incited by Donald Trump and his allies, moved in on the Capitol, resulting in loss of life, many injuries, and gravely threatened our very democracy.

The troubling part of this scenario is that over 70% of white evangelicals doggedly supported this man[39] and continued to support him through this incident. Politics have become deeply ingrained in the American church and I don't know that we will be able to surgically remove them.

It is more likely that the Evangelical Church will doggedly hold to their politics, just like they do to their guns until we pull it from their "cold, dead hand." Occasionally there are signs of hope in these areas, but they are rare.

When I was a Southern Baptist, I used to be appalled and upset when I would hear news of how Catholic priests had molested children and covered it up. But recently, I am hearing the same news about my former denomination, the Southern Baptist Convention.[40]

---

**39** https://www.pewresearch.org/fact-tank/2021/08/30/most-white-americans-who-regularly-attend-worship-services-voted-for-trump-in-2020/

**40** https://www.washingtonpost.com/religion/2022/05/22/southern-baptist-sex-abuse-report/

The stories of cover up at the highest level and victim shaming make me less and less hopeful that it will ever be resolved.

## WHAT IS THE WAY FORWARD?

Keith Giles, who wrote the foreword for this book, has just released a book of his own called *Sola Mysterium: Celebrating the Beautiful Uncertainty of Everything.*[41] In it, he invites us to learn to live with uncertainty as we investigate the mystery of everything.

He challenges us to understand that the opposite of faith is not doubt, it is certainty. Most of our religious problems come when we become certain about what we believe and erected walls and buildings to protect our beliefs, practices, and religion. Many of us have found the glorious delight of living in uncertainty and pursuing the mystery out here in the desert.

## WE ALSO THINK IT IS ESSENTIAL FOR US TO ASK BETTER QUESTIONS

*"The important thing is to never stop questioning."*[42]

We Believe differently than we did 10 years ago. When we honestly let ourselves be curious, we found deeper and better answers. Sometimes the answers were amazingly simple, but often they were nuanced and mysterious and complicated. We are so glad we asked those questions.

---

**41** Giles, Keith. *Sola Mysterium: Celebrating the Beautiful Uncertainty of Everything.* Oak Glen: Quoir, 2022

**42** Einstein, Albert. https://www.brainyquote.com/quotes/albert_einstein_145949

We could have never navigated the stroke recovery with my old understanding.

The key to discovering beauty and truth is to remain curious, not defend what we already know.

We can't solve the problems and challenges of the 21st century with old ideas. We can't cling to beliefs and ideas just because the group we arc familiar with believes that way.

As the world evolves, our understanding of it has to move with it, or we will find ourselves somewhat irrelevant to the world around us."

There are no simple, catchphrase answers anymore. Many of these things are complicated and, when we try to oversimplify them, we end up missing the target completely.

Solving big problems is scary, because we have to leave the comfort zone of our answers, and compromise and cooperate with others to find the best solutions. It's really always been this way—the problems are simply different these days.

We are not asking you to give up anything, but question and consider everything, evolve and if your religion survives, then so be it. If it doesn't survive, then you might not have ever needed it.

We wish you well on your journey,

Be where you are, be who you are,

**—Karl and Laura Forehand**
2022

For more information about Karl and Laura Forehand,

or to contact them for speaking engagements,

please visit *www.KarlForehand.com*

Many voices. One message.